# Data Analysis in the Cloud

# Data Analysis in the Cloud
## Models, Techniques and Applications

Domenico Talia
Paolo Trunfio
Fabrizio Marozzo

AMSTERDAM • BOSTON • HEIDELBERG • LONDON
NEW YORK • OXFORD • PARIS • SAN DIEGO
SAN FRANCISCO • SINGAPORE • SYDNEY • TOKYO

Elsevier
Radarweg 29, PO Box 211, 1000 AE Amsterdam, Netherlands
The Boulevard, Langford Lane, Kidlington, Oxford OX5 1GB, UK
225 Wyman Street, Waltham, MA 02451, USA

ISBN: 978-0-12-802881-0

**British Library Cataloguing-in-Publication Data**
A catalogue record for this book is available from the British Library

**Library of Congress Cataloging-in-Publication Data**
A catalog record for this book is available from the Library of Congress

For information on all Elsevier publications
visit our website at http://store.elsevier.com/

Working together
to grow libraries in
developing countries

www.elsevier.com • www.bookaid.org

# Dedication

*To my beloved parents and to my darling family.*
Domenico Talia

*To my little daughter, Iris, who joined Erika,
Thomas, and me along the way.*
Paolo Trunfio

*To Laura and to my family.*
Fabrizio Marozzo

# CONTENTS

Preface ........................................................................................ xi

**Chapter 1   Introduction to Data Mining** .......................................... 1
1.1 Data Mining Concepts ................................................................... 1
    1.1.1 Classification ....................................................................... 4
    1.1.2 Clustering ............................................................................ 8
    1.1.3 Association Rules ............................................................... 13
1.2 Parallel and Distributed Data Mining ........................................... 16
    1.2.1 Parallel Classification ....................................................... 17
    1.2.2 Parallel Clustering ............................................................. 18
    1.2.3 Parallelism in Association Rules ........................................ 19
    1.2.4 Distributed Data Mining .................................................... 20
1.3 Summary .................................................................................... 23
References ........................................................................................ 24

**Chapter 2   Introduction to Cloud Computing** ................................. 27
2.1 Cloud Computing: Definition, Models, and Architectures ......... 27
    2.1.1 Service Models .................................................................. 28
    2.1.2 Deployment Models ........................................................... 29
    2.1.3 Cloud Environments .......................................................... 32
2.2 Cloud Computing Systems for Data-Intensive Applications ....... 37
    2.2.1 Functional Requirements ................................................... 38
    2.2.2 Nonfunctional Requirements ............................................. 39
    2.2.3 Cloud Models for Distributed Data Analysis .................... 41
2.3 Summary .................................................................................... 43
References ........................................................................................ 43

**Chapter 3   Models and Techniques for Cloud-Based Data Analysis** .... 45
3.1 MapReduce for Data Analysis .................................................... 45
    3.1.1 MapReduce Paradigm ....................................................... 47
    3.1.2 MapReduce Frameworks ................................................... 49
    3.1.3 MapReduce Algorithms and Applications ......................... 51
3.2 Data Analysis Workflows ............................................................ 53

3.2.1 Workflow Programming..................................................55
3.2.2 Workflow Management Systems .............................59
3.2.3 Workflow Management Systems for Clouds ..................61
3.3 NoSQL Models for Data Analytics....................................64
3.3.1 Key Features of NoSQL .............................................64
3.3.2 Classification of NoSQL Databases...........................66
3.3.3 NoSQL Systems.......................................................67
3.3.4 Use Cases................................................................71
3.4 Summary............................................................................72
References............................................................................73

**Chapter 4   Designing and Supporting Scalable Data Analytics .........77**
4.1 Data Analysis Systems for Clouds....................................77
4.1.1 Pegasus .................................................................78
4.1.2 Swift.......................................................................79
4.1.3 Hunk.......................................................................80
4.1.4 Sector/Sphere ........................................................81
4.1.5 BigML .....................................................................82
4.1.6 Kognitio Analytical Platform....................................83
4.1.7 Mahout....................................................................84
4.1.8 Spark ......................................................................85
4.1.9 Microsoft Azure Machine Learning..........................86
4.1.10 ClowdFlows .............................................................87
4.2 How to Design a Scalable Data Analysis Framework in Clouds .....88
4.2.1 Architecture and Execution Mechanisms...........................89
4.2.2 Implementation on Microsoft Azure.............................91
4.3 Programming Workflow-Based Data Analysis .........................92
4.3.1 VL4Cloud .................................................................94
4.3.2 JS4Cloud .................................................................98
4.3.3 Workflow Patterns in DMCF....................................101
4.4 Data Analysis Case Studies .............................................110
4.4.1 Trajectory Mining Workflow Using VL4Cloud................110
4.4.2 Ensemble Learning Workflow Using JS4Cloud .............113
4.4.3 Parallel Classification Using MapReduce in DMCF.......115
4.4.4 Parallel Classification Using Swift .............................118
4.5 Summary............................................................................120
References............................................................................121

**Chapter 5     Research Trends in Big Data Analysis**........................**123**

5.1 Data-Intensive Exascale Computing ........................................ 123

　　5.1.1 Exascale Scalability in Data Analysis............................. 124

　　5.1.2 Programming Issues for Exascale Data Analysis.............. 126

5.2 Massive Social Network Analysis............................................. 130

5.3 Key Research Areas................................................................. 134

5.4 Summary................................................................................. 136

References....................................................................................... 137

The massive amount of digital data currently being generated in all the human activities is a precious source of knowledge to both business and science. However, handling and analyzing huge datasets requires very large storage resources and scalable computing facilities. In fact, the large availability of big data sources demands for efficient data analysis tools and techniques for finding and extracting useful knowledge from them. Big data analysis today can be performed by storing data and running compute-intensive data mining algorithms on cloud computing systems to extract value from data in reduced time. Cloud computing systems can be used to run complex applications on dynamic computing servers and deliver them as services over the Internet. According to their elastic nature, cloud computing infrastructures can serve as effective platforms for addressing the computational and data storage needs of most big data analytics applications that are being developed nowadays. Coping with and gaining value from cloud-based big data, however, requires novel software tools and advanced analysis techniques. Indeed, advanced data mining techniques and innovative tools can help users to understand and extract what is useful in large and complex datasets; and the knowledge extracted from big data sources today is vital in making informed decisions in many business and scientific applications. This process, which constitutes the base for allowing the analysis of big data sources and repositories, must be implemented by combining big data analytics and knowledge discovery techniques with scalable computing systems such as clouds.

All these issues are discussed in this book. In fact, the main goal of the book is to introduce and present models, methods, techniques, and systems useful to analyze large digital data sources by using the computing and storage facilities of cloud computing systems. This book includes, as key topics, scalable data mining and knowledge discovery techniques, together with cloud computing concepts, models, and systems. After introducing these fields, this book focuses on scalable technologies for cloud-based data analysis such as MapReduce, workflows, and NoSQL models, and discusses how to design high-performance distributed analysis of big data on clouds. Finally, this book examines research trends such as big data exascale computing, and massive social network analysis.

This book is for graduate students, researchers, and professionals in cloud computing, big data analysis, distributed data mining, and data analytics. Both readers who are beginners to the subjects and those experienced in the cloud computing and data mining domains will find many topics of interest. Researchers will find some of the latest achievements in the area and significant technologies and examples on the state-of-the-art in cloud-based data analysis and knowledge discovery. Furthermore, graduate students and young researchers will learn useful concepts related to parallel and distributed data mining, cloud computing, data-intensive applications, and scalable data analysis.

Other than introducing the key concepts and systems in the area of cloud-based data analysis, this book presents real case studies that provide a useful guide for developers on issues, prospects, and successful approaches in the practical use of cloud-based data analysis frameworks. In this book, the chapters are presented in a way so that the book could also be used as reference text in graduate and postgraduate courses, in parallel/distributed data mining and in cloud computing for big data analysis.

We would like to thank people from the publisher, Elsevier, particularly Lindsay Lawrence, for their support and work during the book publication process.

We hope readers will find this book's content interesting, attractive, and useful, as we found it stimulating and exciting to write.

Domenico Talia
Paolo Trunfio
Fabrizio Marozzo

# CHAPTER 1

# Introduction to Data Mining

We introduce in this chapter the main concepts of data mining. This scientific field, together with Cloud computing, discussed in Chapter 2, is a basic pillar on which the contents of this book are built. Section 1.1 explores the main notions and principles of data mining introducing readers to this scientific field and giving them the needed information on sequential data mining techniques and algorithms that will be used in other sections and chapters of this book. Section 1.2 outlines the most important parallel and distributed data mining strategies and techniques.

## 1.1 DATA MINING CONCEPTS

Computers have been created to help humans in executing complex and long operations automatically. One of the main effects of the invention of computers is the very huge amount of digital data that nowadays is stored in the memory of computers. Those data volumes can be used to know and understand facts, behaviors, and natural phenomena and take decisions on the basis of them. Researchers investigated methods for instructing computers to learn from data. In particular, machine learning is a scientific discipline that deals with the design and implementation of models, procedures, and algorithms that can learn from data. Such techniques are able to build a predictive model based on data input to be used for making predictions or taking decisions. More recently, data mining has been defined as an area of computer science where machine learning techniques are used to discover previously *unknown* properties in large data sets. More formally, data mining is the analysis of data sets to find interesting, novel, and useful patters, relationships, models, and trends. Data mining tasks include methods at the intersection of artificial intelligence, machine learning, statistics, mathematics, and database systems. The overall practical goal of a data mining task is to extract information from a data set and transform it into an understandable structure for further use. Data mining is considered also the central step of the knowledge discovery in databases (KDD) process that aims at discovering useful patterns and models for making sense of data. The additional steps in the KDD process are data preparation, data selection, data cleaning, incorporation of appropriate prior knowledge, and interpretation of the results of mining. They are essential to ensure, together with the data mining step, that useful knowledge is derived from the data that have to be analyzed.

Many data mining algorithms have been designed and implemented in several research areas such as statistics, machine learning, mathematics, artificial intelligence, pattern recognition, and databases, each of which uses specialized techniques from the respective application field. The most common types of data mining tasks include:

- *Classification*: the goal is to classify a data set in one or more predefined classes. This is done by models that implement a mapping from a vector of values to a categorical variable. In this way using classification we can predict the membership of a data instance to a given class from a set of predefined classes. For instance, a set of outlet store clients can be grouped in three classes: high spending, average spending, and low spending clients or a set of patients can be classified according to a set of diseases. Classification techniques are used in many application domains such financial services, bioinformatics, document classification, multimedia data, text processing, and social network analysis.
- *Regression*: it is a predictive technique that associates a data set to a quantitative variable and predicts the value of that variable. There are many applications of regression, such as assessing the likelihood that a patient can get sick from the results of diagnostic tests, predicting the margin of victory of a sport team based on results and technical data of previous matches. Regression is often used in economics, environmental studies, market trends, meteorology, and epidemiology.
- *Clustering*: this data mining task is targeted to identify a finite set of categories or groupings (clusters) to describe the data. Clustering techniques are used when no class to be predicted is available *a priori* and data instances are to be divided in groups of similar instances. The groups can be mutually exclusive and exhaustive, or consist of a more extensive representation, such as in the case of hierarchical

categories. Examples of clustering applications concern the finding of homogeneous subsets of clients in a database of commercial sales or groups of objects with similar shapes and colors. Among the application domains where clustering is used are gene analysis, network intrusion, medical imaging, crime analysis, climatology, and text mining. Unlike classification in which classes are predefined, in clustering the classes must be derived from data, looking for clusters based on metrics of similarity between data without the assistance of users.

- *Summarization*: this data mining task provides a compact description of a subset of data. Summarization methods for unstructured data usually involve text classification that groups together documents sharing similar characteristics. An example of summarization of quantitative data is the tabulation of the mean and standard deviation of each data field. More complex functions involve summary rules and the discovery of functional relationships between variables. Summarization techniques are often used in the interactive analysis of data and the automatic generation of reports.

- *Dependency modeling*: this task consists in finding a model that describes significant dependencies between variables. Here the goal is to discover how some data values depend on other data values. Dependency models are at two levels: the structural level of the model specifies which variables are locally dependent on each other, while the quantitative level specifies the power of dependencies using a numeric scale. Dependency modeling approaches are used in retail, business process management, software development, and assembly line optimization.

- *Association rule discovery*: this task aims at finding sets of items that occur together in records of a data set and the relationships among those items in order to derive multiple correlations that meet the specified thresholds. It is intended to identify strong rules discovered in large data sets using different measures of interestingness. In several application domains it is useful to know how often two or more items of interest co-occur. For instance, association rules can describe which products are commonly sold with other products in one or more stores. In this case association analysis is sometimes called *market basket analysis*. Other significant domains where association discovery is used are web page access, communication

network usage, credit card services, medical diagnosis, and
bioinformatics.

- *Outlier detection:* an outlier, is one observation or an item that
  appears to be inconsistent with or deviate significantly from
  other items of a data set in which it occurs. Although an outlier
  can be considered as an error or noise, outliers carry important
  information. Outlier detection methods have been proposed for
  several application domains, such as weather prediction, credit card
  fraud detection, clinical trials, network intrusion detection, system
  performance analysis, and other data analysis problems.
- *Episode discovery* or *prediction*: this task looks for relationships
  between temporal sequences of events. Data instances are viewed
  as sequences of events, where each event has an associated time of
  occurrence. One key problem in analyzing event sequences is to find
  frequent episodes, that is, collections of events occurring frequently
  together. For example, finding that if a given event $E_1$ happens,
  then, within a time interval *t,* there will be also an event $E_2$ with
  probability *p*. Examples of domains where to use episode discovery
  are alarm analysis in telecommunications, web log analysis, client
  action sequences, fault analysis in manufacturing plants, occurrences
  of weather events.

## 1.1.1 Classification

A classification task has the goal to predict the class for a given unlabeled item. The class must be selected among a finite set of predefined
classes. Classification algorithms are among the most used techniques in
data mining tasks because in many application domains, data associated
to class label are available. In all these cases, a classification algorithm
can build a classifier that is a model *M* that calculates the class label *c*
for a given input item *x*, that is, $c = M(x)$, where $c \in \{c_1, c_2, ..., c_n\}$ and
each $c_i$ is a class label. To build the model the algorithm requires a set
of available items together with their correct class label. This set of classified items is called the *training set*. After generating the model *M*, the
classifier can automatically predict the class for any new item that will be
given as input to it. Several classification models have been introduced
such as decision trees, statistical classifiers, k-nearest neighbors, support
vector machines, neural networks, and others. In this section we introduce decision trees and k-nearest neighbors.

### 1.1.1.1 Decision Trees

Decision trees are the most developed methods for partitioning sets of items into classes. A decision tree classifies data items into a finite number of predefined classes. The tree nodes are labeled with the names of attributes, the arcs are labeled with the possible values of the attribute, and the leaves are labeled with the different classes. Decision trees were introduced in the Quinlan's (1986) ID3 system, one of the earliest data mining algorithms. An item is classified by following a path along the tree formed by the arcs corresponding to the values of its attributes.

A descendant of ID3 used often today for building decision trees is C4.5 (Quinlan, 1993). Given a set $C$ of items, C4.5 first grows a decision tree using the divide-and-conquer algorithm as follows:

- If all the items in $C$ belong to the same class or $C$ is small, the tree is a leaf labeled with the most frequent class in $C$.
- Otherwise, choose a test based on a single attribute with two or more outcomes. Make this test the root of the tree with one branch for each outcome of the test, partition $C$ into a collection of subsets $C_1$, $C_2$, ..., $C_n$ according to the outcome for each item, and apply the same procedure recursively to each subset.

Several tests could be used in this last step. C4.5 uses two heuristic criteria to rank possible tests: information gain, which minimizes the total entropy of the subsets $\{C_i\}$, and the default gain ratio that divides information gain by the information provided by the test outcomes.

Attributes can be either numeric or nominal and this determines the format of the test outcomes. For a numeric attribute $A$ they are $\{A \leq t, A > t\}$ where the threshold $t$ is found by sorting $C$ on the values of $A$ and choosing the split between successive values that maximizes the criterion above. An attribute $A$ with discrete values has by default one outcome for each value, but an option allows the values to be grouped into two or more subsets with one outcome for each subset.

The initial tree is then pruned to avoid overfitting. The pruning algorithm is based on a pessimistic estimate of the error rate associated with a set of $N$ cases, $Z$ of which do not belong to the most frequent class. Instead of $Z/N$, C4.5 determines the upper limit of the binomial probability when $Z$ events have been observed in $N$ trials, using a user-specified confidence whose default value is 0.25.

Pruning is performed starting from the leaves towards the root. The estimated error at a leaf with $N$ items and $Z$ errors is $N$ times the pessimistic error rate as above. For a subtree, C4.5 adds the estimated errors of the branches and compares it to the estimated error if, the subtree is replaced by a leaf. If the latter is no higher than the former, the subtree is pruned. Similarly, C4.5 checks the estimated error if the subtree is replaced by one of its branches and when this appears beneficial the tree is modified accordingly. The pruning process is completed in one pass through the tree.

A disadvantage of decision trees is that they grow too much in real-world data mining applications therefore they become difficult to understand. Research efforts have been carried out to find simpler representations for decision trees.

In classification techniques based on decision-tree generation such as C4.5 have introduced methods to generate production rules from decision trees. The experts because of their high modularity easily interpret production rules. Each rule can be understood without reference to other rules. The accuracy of classification of a decision tree can be improved by transforming the tree into a set of production rules that contain a smaller number of attribute-value conditions. In fact, some conditions may be redundant and Quinlan (1987) showed that their removal reduces the rate of misclassification on the examples that are not part of the training set.

A simple example of a set of classification rules that allow to classify driver license in some US states are as follows:

*if Age > 14 and Age < 18 and family = suffering then*
*class = Hardship*
*if Age ≥ 16 and Age < 18 and family = regular then*
*class = Provisional*
*default class = Unrestricted*

This classification rule set states that *hardship* licenses for minors are restricted to people between 14 and 18 years old who need to drive to/from home and school due to serious hardships. Provisional licenses are issued to new drivers between 14 and 18 years old. The remaining (most Americans) drivers have unrestricted driver licenses.

As Wu et al. (2008) reported in their survey, the main disadvantage of classification rules like the ones produced by C4.5, is the amount of computing time and memory size that they require. In an experiment, data samples ranging from 10,000 to 100,000 items were drawn from a large data set. For decision trees, including from 10,000 to 100,000 items CPU time on a PC increased from 1.4 s to 61 s. The time required for rulesets, however, increased from 32 s to 9715 s (more than 300 times).

### 1.1.1.2 Classification with kNN

An effective and composite algorithm for data classification is the so-called *k-nearest neighbor* (kNN) classification (Fix and Hodges, 1951), which finds a group of $k$ objects in the training set that are closest to the test object, and bases the assignment of a label on the predominance of a particular class in this neighborhood. This allows, for example to find people who have similar financial status to give them similar credit ratings, or to predict the variety of a plant based on the similarity of its characteristics with predefined set of plant samples.

There are three main elements of this technique:

- a set of labeled items, for example a set of records;
- a distance metric or similarity metric to calculate the distance among objects; and
- the value of $k$, that is the number of nearest neighbors.

To classify an unlabeled data item, the distance of this item to the labeled items is calculated, its $k$-nearest neighbors are identified, then the class labels of these nearest neighbors are used to select the class label of the item.

In particular, the nearest-neighbor classification algorithm operates as follows. Given a training set $T$ and a test item $i = (d', f')$, where $d'$ is the data attributes of the test item and $f'$ is the item class, the algorithm computes the similarity between $i$ and all the training items $(d, f)$ $\in T$ to determine its nearest-neighbor list, $T_i$. Notice that $d$ represents the data attributes of the training item and $f$ is the item class. Once the nearest-neighbor list is obtained, the test object is classified based on the majority class of its nearest neighbors:

$$f' = \arg\max_c \sum_{(d_j, f_j) \in T_i} F(c = f_i)$$

where $c$ is a class label, $f_j$ is the class label for the $j$th nearest neighbors, and $F(\cdot)$ is an indicator function that returns 1 if its argument is true and 0 otherwise. The kNN technique has been used in many application fields such as: text and document retrieval, bioinformatics, image processing, marketing data analysis, video analysis, and multimedia databases.

The following very simple example shows how the kNN algorithms classifies the rows of the matrix $M$ composed of three rows and two columns. Having $M = [0.90\ 0.86;0.10\ 0.31;0.28\ 0.40]$ and using the following training set $TR = [0\ 0;0.5\ 0.4;0.8\ 1.0]$, where row 1 defines class 1, row 2 defines class 2, and row 3 defines class 3, the classes of the rows of $M$ are obtained as follows: row 1 of $M$ is closest to row 3 of $TR$, so class(1) = 3. Row 2 of $M$ is closest to row 1 of $TR$ so class(2) = 1, and row 3 of $M$ is closest to row 2 of $TR$, so class(3) = 2.

## 1.1.2 Clustering

Clustering is an unsupervised learning technique that separates data items into a number of groups or clusters such that items in the same cluster are more similar to each other and items in different clusters tend to be dissimilar, according to some measure of similarity or proximity. Differently from supervised learning, where training examples are associated with a class label that expresses the membership of every example to a class, clustering assumes no information about the distribution of the items, and it has the task to both discover the classes present in the data set and to assign items among such classes in the best way.

Clustering algorithms can roughly be classified into the three following types (Everitt, 1977): *hierarchical*, *partitional* and *density* or *mode-seeking*.

*Hierarchical methods* generate a nested sequence of clusters by a hierarchical decomposition of a set of $N$ objects represented by a *dendrogram*. To build the dendrogram, there are two techniques, which work in opposite directions: the *agglomerative* and the *divisive*. Agglomerative methods start with the $N$ items and at each step two clusters are merged until only one is left. Divisive methods, on the contrary, start with one single cluster containing all the items and iteratively a cluster is split until $N$ clusters containing a single item are obtained. Well-known hierarchical methods are BIRCH, CURE, and CHAMELEON. *Partitional methods* produce a partition of a set of items into $K$ clusters by optimizing a given criterion function. One of the most known criterion is the *squared error criterion*. The *K-means* clustering (Kaufman and Rousseeuw, 1990) is a well-known and effective method for many practical applications that employ the squared error criterion. *Density search techniques* consider items as points in a metric space and suggest that clusters should be those parts of the space characterized by a high density of data. High-density regions are called *modes*. In Everitt (1977) several density-seeking methods are reported.

Statistical density search-based approaches consider dense regions of the probability density of the data items as different groups. This approach uses statistical concepts with the aim to represent the probability density function through a mixture model. A mixture model consists of several components such that each component generates a cluster. The problem in the mixture model framework is to find the characteristics of the data distribution in each cluster. The *Expectation-Maximization* (*EM*) algorithm of Dempster et al. (1977) and Titterington et al. (1985) is a well-known technique for estimating mixture model parameters that iteratively refines initial mixture model parameter estimates. Several implementations of the *EM* algorithm have been provided and the benefits of this approach with respect to other methods have been analyzed. The method is proved to be scalable on large databases and outperforms the traditional scaling approaches based on sampling.

### 1.1.2.1 Bayesian Classification

The Bayesian approach to unsupervised learning provides a probabilistic method to inductive inference. In Bayesian classification class membership is expressed probabilistically that is an item is not assigned to a unique class, instead it has a probability of belonging to each of the possible classes. The classes provide probabilities for all attribute values of each item. Class membership probabilities are then determined by combining all these probabilities. Class membership probabilities of each item must sum to 1, thus there are not precise boundaries for classes: every item must be a member of some class, even though we do not know which one. When every item has a probability of no more than 0.5 in any class, the classification is not well defined because it means that classes are abundantly overlapped. On the contrary, when the probability of each instance is about 0.99 in its most probable class, the classes are well separated.

Let $D = \{X_1,...X_m\}$ denotes the observed data objects, where instances or items $X_i$ are represented as ordered vectors of attribute values $X_i = \{X_{i1},..., X_{ik}\}$. Unsupervised classification aims at determining the *best* class description (hypothesis) $h$ from some space $H$ that predicts data $D$. The term *best* can be interpreted as the *most probable* hypothesis given the observed data $D$ and some prior knowledge on the hypotheses of $H$ in the absence of $D$, that is the prior probabilities of the various hypotheses in $H$ when no data have been observed. Bayes theorem provides a way to compute the probabilities of the best hypothesis, given the prior probabilities, the probabilities of observing the data given the various hypotheses and the observed data.

Let $P(h)$ denote the *prior probability* that the hypothesis $h$ holds before the data have been observed. Analogously, let $P(D)$ denote the prior probability that the data will be observed, that is the probability of $D$ with no knowledge of which hypothesis holds. $P(D|h)$ denotes the probability of observing $D$ in some world where the hypothesis $h$ is valid. In unsupervised classification the main problem is to find the probability $P(h|D)$, that is the probability that the hypothesis $h$ is valid, given the observed data $D$. $P(h|D)$ is called the *posterior probability* of $h$ and expresses the degree of belief in $h$ after the data have been seen. Thus the set of data items biases the posterior probability, while the prior probability is independent of $D$. Bayes theorem provides a method to compute the posterior probability:

$$P(h|D) = \frac{P(D|h)P(h)}{P(D)}$$

which is equivalent to

$$P(h|D) = \frac{P(D|h)P(h)}{\sum_h P(D|h)P(h)}$$

because of the theorem of total probability which asserts that if events $h_1$, ..., $h_n$ are mutually exclusive with $\sum_{i=1}^{n} P(h_i) = 1$ then $P(D) = \sum_{i=1}^{n} P(D \mid h_i) P(h_i)$.

When the set of possible $h$ is continuous then the prior becomes a differential and the sums over $h$ are integrals, thus this computation becomes difficult to realize. The undertaken approach consists in using approximations in the following way. Instead of considering all the possible states of the world and, consequently all the possible hypotheses $h$ specifying that the world is in some particular state, in *EM* only a small space of models is considered and the assumption *S* that one of such models describes the world is believed true. A model consists of two sets of parameters: *a set of discrete parameters* *T* which describes the functional form of the model, such as number of classes and whether attributes are correlated, and *a set of continuous parameters* *V* that specifies values for the variables appearing in *T*, needed to complete the general form of the model. Given a set of data *D*, *EM* searches for the most probable pair *V, T* which classifies *D*, $P(D\ V\ T \mid S) = P(D \mid V\ T\ S) P(V\ T \mid S)$. This is done in two steps:

1. For a given *T*, *EM* seeks the maximum posterior (*MAP*) parameter values *V*.
2. Regardless of any *V*, *EM* searches for the most probable *T*, from a set of possible $T_s$ with different attribute dependencies and class structure.

There are two levels of search: *parameter level search* and *model level search*. Fixed the number *J* of classes and their class model, the space of allowed parameter values is searched for finding the most probable *V*. This space is real valued and contains many local maxima, thus finding the global maximum is not an easy task. The algorithm randomly generates a starting point and converges on the maximal values nearest to the starting point. Model level search chooses the best model structure. It is assumed that all instances in *D* are independent, thus

$$P(D \mid VTS) = \prod_i P(X_i \mid VTS)$$

and it is necessary to find the probability $P(X_i \mid VTS)$ of each instance $X_i$.

The joint probability $P(DVT|S)$ has, generally, many local maxima. To find them, a variant of the $EM$ algorithm of Dempster et al. (1977) and Titterington et al. (1985) implemented in *AutoClass*, is based on the fact that at a maximum the class parameter $V_j$ can be estimated from *weighted sufficient statistics*, that summarizes all the information relevant to a model. The weights $w_{ij}$ give the probability that an instance $X_i$ is a member of class $j$. These weights must satisfy $\Sigma_j\ w_{ij} = 1$. This approximate information can be used to re-estimate the parameters $V$ and this new set of parameters permits re-estimation of the class probabilities. Repeating these two steps brings to a local optimum. In order to find as many local maxima as possible, *Auto-Class* generates pseudorandom points in the parameter space, converges to a local optimum, records the results and repeats the same steps.

### 1.1.2.2 The K-Means Algorithm

$K$-means is one of the most used clustering algorithms based on a *partitional strategy*. $K$-means is an algorithm that minimizes the squared error of values from their respective cluster means. In this way $K$-means implements hard clustering, where each item is assigned to only one cluster (Kaufman and Rousseeeuw, 1990). On the contrary, $EM$ is a soft clustering approach because it returns the probability that an item belongs to each cluster. Thus $EM$ can be seen as a generalization of $K$-means obtained by modeling the data as a mixture of normal distributions, and finding the cluster parameters (the mean and covariance matrix) by maximizing the likelihood of data.

The $K$-means algorithm is an iterative clustering algorithm to partition a given dataset into a user specified number of clusters, $k$. The algorithm has been proposed by several researchers such as Lloyd (1957, 1982), Friedman and Rubin (1967), and McQueen (1967).

The algorithm operates on a set of $d$-dimensional vectors, $D = \{x_i\ |\ i = 1,\ldots, N\}$, where $x_i$ is a real vector, so it belongs to $\mathfrak{R}^d$ and denotes the $i$th data item. The algorithm starts by picking $k$ points in $\mathfrak{R}^d$ as the initial representatives or "centroids" of the $k$ clusters. Several techniques for selecting these initial seeds have been proposed. They include sampling at random from the dataset, setting them as the solution of clustering a small subset of the data or perturbing the global mean of the data $k$ times. Then the algorithm iterates between two steps till it will converge:

$S1$ – *Assignment Step*: Each data item is assigned to its *nearest* centroid (whose mean yields the least within-cluster sum of squares), with ties broken arbitrarily. This results in a partitioning of the data set in **k** groups or clusters.

*S2 – Relocation Step*: The new means to be the centroids of the observations in the new clusters are calculated. Each cluster representative is relocated to the center (mean) of all data items assigned to it. If the data items have an associated probability measure (weights), then the relocation is to the expectations (weighted mean) of the data partitions.

The *K*-means algorithm converges when the assignments (and hence the $c_j$ values) no longer change. Notice that each iteration needs $N \times k$ comparisons, which determines the time complexity of one iteration. The number of iterations required for convergence varies and can depend on $N$, but as a first cut, this algorithm can be considered linear in the dataset size.

One issue to solve is how to quantify the nearest concept in the assignment step. The default measure of closeness is the Euclidean distance, in which case one can readily show that the nonnegative cost function below will decrease whenever there is a change in the assignment or the relocation steps, and hence convergence is guaranteed in a finite number of iterations.

$$\sum_{i=1}^{N} \left( \underset{j}{\mathrm{argmin}} \left\| x_i - c_j \right\|_2^2 \right)$$

As can be deduced from the assignment step, the *K*-means algorithm is sensitive to initialization, and it suffers from other limitations. For example, the algorithm works well when the data fits the cluster model, that is the clusters are spherical because the data points in a cluster are centered around that cluster, and the spread/variance of the clusters is similar, that is each data point belongs to the closest cluster. Despite those limitation, the *K*-means is the most used clustering algorithm.

### 1.1.3 Association Rules

As we mentioned before, in many application domains it is useful to discover how often two or more items co-occur. This holds, for example, when we wish to know what goods customers buy together or which pages of a web site users access in the same session. Mining frequent patters is the basic task in all these cases. Once the frequent groups of items are found in a data set, it is also possible to discover the association rules that hold for the frequent itemsets. Association rule discovery has been proposed by Agrawal et al. (1993) as a method for discovering interesting association among variables in large data sets.

The association rule mining task can be defined as follows: Let $I = \{i_1, i_2, ..., i_n\}$ be a set of $n$ binary attributes called *items*. Let $D = \{t_1, t_2, ..., t_m\}$ be a set of transactions called the *data set*. Each transaction in $D$ has a unique transaction identifier and contains a subset of the items in $I$ called *itemset*. A *rule* is defined as an implication of the form

$$X \Rightarrow Y \qquad \text{where } X, Y \subseteq I \text{ and } X \cap Y = \emptyset.$$

The *itemsets* $X$ and $Y$ are called *antecedent* and *consequent* of the rule, respectively. The antecedent and consequent are sets of items that are disjoint. A simple example rule for a set of products sold in a supermarket in the same basket of a client could be *(mustard, Vienna sausages)* $\Rightarrow$ *(buns)* meaning that if customers buy mustard and hot dog sausages, they also buy buns.

The degree of uncertainty of an association rule is expressed by two values. The first one is called the *support* for the rule. The *support* is the number of transactions that include all items in the antecedent and consequent parts of the rule. The *support* can be expressed as relative value, that is a percentage of the total number of records in the data set. For example, if an itemset {*mustard, Vienna sausages, buns*} occurs in 25% of all transactions (1 out of 4 transactions), it has a *support* of 1/4 = 0.25. The second value is known as the *confidence* of the rule. The *confidence* is the ratio of the number of transactions that include all items in the consequent as well as the antecedent (the *support*) to the number of transactions that include all items in the antecedent: *confidence*($X \Rightarrow Y$) = *support*($X \cup Y$) / *support*($X$). For example, if a supermarket database has 100,000 transactions, out of which 5,000 include both items $X$ and $Y$ and 1,000 of these include item $Z$, the association rule "If $X$ and $Y$ are purchased, then $Z$ is purchased in the same basket" has a support of 1,000 transactions (alternatively 2% = 1,000/100,000) and a *confidence* of 20% (=1,000/5,000).

Association rules are usually searched to satisfy user-specified *minimum support* and *minimum confidence* at the same time. Association rule generation is usually split up into two separate steps:

1. Minimum support is applied to find all frequent itemsets in a data set.
2. These frequent itemsets and the minimum confidence constraint are used to compose the rules.

Finding all frequent itemsets in a data set is a complex procedure since it involves analyzing all possible itemsets. All the possible itemsets is the power set over $I$ and has size $2^{n-1}$ (excluding the empty set which is not a valid itemset). Although the size of the power set grows exponentially in the number of items $n$ in $I$, efficient search is possible using the *downward-closure property* of support (also called *antimonotonicity*) which guarantees that for a frequent itemset, all its subsets are also frequent, therefore for an infrequent itemset, all its supersets must also be infrequent. Efficient algorithms such as Apriori (Agrawal and Srikant, 1994) and Eclat (Zaki, 2000) can find all frequent itemsets.

In particular, Apriori is one of the most used algorithms for finding frequent itemsets using candidate generation. It is characterized as a level-wise search algorithm using *antimonotonicity* of itemsets. Let the set of frequent itemsets of size $k$ be $F_k$ and their candidates be $C_k$. Apriori first scans the database and searches for frequent itemsets of size 1 by counting the occurrence of each item and collecting those that satisfy the minimum support requirement. It then iterates on the following three steps and extracts all the frequent itemsets.

1. Generate $C_{k+1}$, candidates of frequent itemsets of size $k + 1$, from the frequent itemsets of size $k$.
2. Scan the database and calculate the support of each candidate of frequent itemsets.
3. Add those itemsets that satisfy the minimum support requirement to $F_{k+1}$.

In general, the Apriori algorithm gets good performance by reducing the size of candidate sets; however, when must be analyzed very many frequent itemsets, large itemsets, and/or very low minimum support is used, Apriori suffers from the cost of generating a huge number of candidate sets and for scanning all the transactions repeatedly to check a large set of candidate itemsets. For example, it is necessary to generate $2^{80}$ candidate itemsets to obtain frequent itemsets of size 80. For this reason, more efficient sequential and parallel solutions for frequent itemset mining have been designed to handle large and very frequent itemsets.

## 1.2 PARALLEL AND DISTRIBUTED DATA MINING

This section introduces the main strategies that are used for the implementation of parallel and distributed data mining techniques and describes a few parallel data mining algorithms. Sequential data mining algorithms designed to analyze very large and/or distributed data sets on conventional computers often need to run for a very long time to produce the data mining models. The main approach to reduce response time is to use parallel and distributed computing models and systems. High performance computers, such as multiclusters, clouds, and many-core systems, if equipped with distributed and parallel data mining tools and algorithms, can provide an effective approach to analyze big data sets and obtain results in reasonable time. This approach is based on the exploitation of inherent parallelism of most data mining algorithms. Here we introduce the main issues and discuss some solutions.

Three main strategies can be identified for the exploitation of parallelism in data mining algorithms:

- *Independent parallelism*: it can be exploited when processes are executed in parallel in a fully independent way. Generally, each process accesses the whole data set and does not communicate or synchronize with other processes during the data mining operations.
- *Single Program Multiple Data* (*SPMD*) *parallelism*: a set of processes execute in parallel the same algorithm on different partitions of a data set; processes cooperate to exchange partial results during execution.
- *Task/control parallelism*: it is the more general form of parallelism since each process can execute different operations on (a different partition of) the data set, and processes communicate as the parallel algorithm requires.

It must be noted that the three models are not necessarily alternative for the implementation of parallel data mining algorithms. They can be combined to implement hybrid parallel data mining algorithms (Talia, 2002).

## 1.2.1 Parallel Classification

As described in Section 1.1.1.1, decision trees are an effective and popular technique for classification. They are tree-shaped structures that represent a way to classify items. Paths in those trees, from the root to a leaf, correspond to rules for classifying a data set whereas the tree leaves represent the classes and the tree nodes represent attribute values.

*Independent parallelism* can be exploited in decision tree construction assigning to a process the goal to construct a decision tree according to some parameters. If several processes are executed in parallel on different computing elements, a set of decision tree classifiers can be obtained at the same time. One or more of such trees can be selected as classifiers for the data.

Using the *Task parallelism approach* one process is associated to each subtree of the decision tree that is built to represent a classification model. The search occurs in parallel in each subtree, thus the degree of parallelism $P$ is equal to the number of active processes at a given time. This approach can be implemented using the farm parallelism pattern in which one master process controls the computation and a set of $W$ workers that are assigned to the subtrees. The result is a single decision tree built in a shorter time with respect to the sequential tree building.

According to *SPMD parallelism*, a set of processes executes the same code to classify the items of a subset of the data set. The $P$ processes search in parallel in the whole tree using a partition $D/P$ of the data set $D$. The global result is obtained by exchanging partial results among the processes. The data set partitioning may be operated in two different ways: (i) by partitioning the $D$ tuples of the data set assigning $D/P$ tuples per processor or (ii) by partitioning the $n$ attributes of each tuple and assigning $D$ tuples of $n/P$ attributes per processor.

Kufrin (1997) proposed a parallel implementation of the C4.5 algorithm that uses the independent parallelism approach. Some other examples of parallel algorithms for building decision trees are Top-Down Induction of Decision Trees (Pearson, 1994) and SPRINT (Shafer et al., 1996).

## 1.2.2 Parallel Clustering

Parallelism in clustering algorithms can be exploited both in the data clustering strategy and in the computation of the similarity or distance among the data items by computing on each processor the distance/similarity of a different partition of items. In the parallel implementation of clustering algorithms the three main parallel strategies described before can be used.

In *Independent parallelism* each processor uses the whole data set $D$ and implements a different clustering task based on a different number of clusters $k_p$. To get the load among the processors balanced, until the clustering task is complete a new clustering task is assigned to a processor that completed its assigned grouping.

According to *Task parallelism* each processor executes a different task that executes the clustering algorithm and cooperates with the other processors exchanging partial results. For example, in partitioning methods processors can work on disjoint regions of the search space using the whole data set. In hierarchical methods a processor can be responsible of composing one or more clusters. It finds the nearest neighbor cluster by computing the distance among its cluster and the others. Then all the local shortest distances are exchanged to find the global shortest distance between two clusters that must be merged. The new cluster will be assigned to one of the two processors that handled the merged clusters.

Finally, in *SPMD parallelism* each processor run the same algorithm on a different partition $D/P$ of the data set to compute partial clustering results. Local results obtained on the assigned partitions are then shared among all the processors to compute global values on every processor. Global values are used in all processors to start the next clustering step until a convergence is reached or a given number of clustering steps are performed. The SPMD strategy can also be used to implement clustering algorithms where each processor generates a local approximation of a model, which at each iteration can be sent to the other processors that in turn use it to improve their clustering model.

A parallel implementation of a clustering algorithm is, for example, P-CLUSTER. Other parallel algorithms are discussed in Bruynooghe (1989) and Foti et al. (2000). In particular, in Pizzuti and Talia (2003) an SPMD implementation of the AutoClass algorithm, named P-AutoClass is described. That paper shows interesting performance results on distributed memory MIMD machines. Finally, Olson (1995) presents a set of hierarchical clustering algorithms and an analysis of their time complexity on different parallel architectures.

### 1.2.3 Parallelism in Association Rules

As discussed, association rules algorithms are used for the automatic discovery of complex associations in a data set. Given a set of transactions $D$, as described in Section 1.1.3, the problem of mining association rules is to generate all association rules that have support (how often a combination occurred overall) and confidence (how often the association rule holds true in the data set) greater than the user-specified minimum support and minimum confidence respectively.

*Independent parallelism* can be used to run in parallel association rule algorithms that avoid data dependencies among the different processes. This can be done by partitioning and replicating data and candidate frequent itemsets so that processes can run autonomously. For example the Candidate Distribution method proposed for implementing the Apriori algorithm (Agrawal and Shafer, 1996) partitions candidate itemsets but selectively replicates instead of partition-and-exchanging the database transactions, so that each process can proceed independently.

In *SPMD parallelism* the data set $D$ is partitioned among the $P$ processors but candidate itemsets $I$ are replicated on each processor. Each process $p$ counts in parallel the partial support $S_p$ of the global itemsets on its local partition of the data set of size $D/P$. At the end of this phase the global support $S$ is obtained by collecting all local supports $S_p$. The replication of the candidate itemsets minimizes communication, but it does not use memory efficiently. Due to low communication overhead, scalability is good.

According to *Task parallelism*, both the data set $D$ and the candidate itemsets $I$ are partitioned on each processor. Each process $p$ counts the global support $S_i$ of its candidate itemset $I_p$ on the entire data set $D$. After scanning its local data set partition $D/P$, a process must scan all remote partitions for each iteration. The partitioning of the data set and the candidate itemsets minimizes the use of memory but requires high communication overhead in distributed memory architectures. Due to communication overhead this approach is less scalable than the previous one.

Also in this case, a combination of the three different parallelism approaches can be implemented. As mentioned, the Apriori algorithm is the most known algorithm for association rules discovery. Several parallel implementations have been proposed for this algorithm. In (Agrawal and Shafer, 1996) three different parallel algorithms called Count Distribution, Data Distribution, and Candidate Distribution are presented. The first one is based on SPMD parallelism, the second one is based on task parallelism whereas the third one, as stated above, uses the independent parallelism approach. In Han et al. (2000) two additional parallel approaches to Apriori called Intelligent Data Distribution (IDD) and Hybrid Distribution (HD) are presented. A complete review of parallel algorithms for association rules can be found in Zaki (1999).

### 1.2.4 Distributed Data Mining

*Distributed data mining* (DDM) techniques use distributed computing systems to store data sets and run data mining algorithms exploiting their inherent parallelism by distributing data on different computers and running the mining code locally on that computers. This approach is suitable for applications that typically deal with very large amount of data that cannot be analyzed in a single computer or on a single site using traditional machines in acceptable times or that need to mine data sources located in remote sites, such as Web servers or departmental data owned by large enterprises, or data streams coming from sensor networks or satellites.

Centralized architectures are inappropriate for most of the distributed and ubiquitous data mining applications that involve the processing of Big Data. In fact, the long response time, the lack of proper use of distributed resource, and the fundamental features of centralized data mining algorithms do not work well in parallel and distributed environments. As we discussed for parallel data analysis techniques, scalable solutions for distributed applications calls for distributed processing of data, controlled by the available resources and expert data miners.

Most distributed data analysis algorithms are designed upon the potential concurrency they can apply over the given distributed data.

Typically, the same code runs on each distributed data site concurrently, producing one local model per site. Subsequently, all local models are aggregated to produce the final model. This schema is common to several distributed data mining algorithms. Among them, ensemble learning, meta-learning, and collective data mining are the most important. Moreover, we must mention that distribution and parallelism can also be used together to implement very large distributed data analysis applications where also the local models that compose the global model obtained in a distributed way, are computed in parallel according to the techniques discussed in the previous section.

### 1.2.4.1 Meta-Learning

The meta-learning techniques aim at implementing a global model from a set of distributed data sets. Meta-learning can be defined as learning from learned knowledge (Prodromidis et al., 2000). In a data classification scenario, this is achieved by learning from the predictions of a set of base data classifiers on a common validation set. Here we list the steps needed to build a global classifier from a set of distributed training sets according to a meta-learning approach:

1. The initial training sets are given in input to $n$ learning algorithms that run in parallel to build $n$ classification models (base classifiers).
2. A meta-level training set is built by combining the predictions of the base classifiers on a common validation set.
3. A global classifier is trained from the meta-level training set by a meta-learning algorithm.

*Stacking* is a way of combining multiple models in meta-learning. Stacking is not used to combine models of the same type. It is applied to models built by using different learning algorithms. It does not use a voting approach, but tries to learn which classifiers are the reliable ones, using another learning algorithm (the meta-learner) to discover how best to combine the output of the base learners.

### 1.2.4.2 Collective Data Mining

Collective data mining, instead of combining a set of complete models generated at each site on partitioned or replicated data sets, builds the global model through the combination of partial models computed in the different sites. The global model is directly composed by summing an appropriate set of basis functions. The global function $f(x)$ that represents the global model can be expressed as:

$$f(x) = \sum_k w_k \, \psi_k(x)$$

where $\psi_k(x)$ is the $k$th basis function and $w_k$ is the corresponding coefficient that must be learned locally on each site based on the stored data set. This result is founded on the fact that any function can be expressed in a distributed fashion using a set of appropriate basis functions that may contain nonlinear terms. If the basis functions are orthonormal, the local analysis generates results that can be correctly used as components of the global model. If in the summation function is present a nonlinear term, the global model is not fully decomposable among local sites and crossterms involving features from different sites must be considered. Kargupta et al. (2000), described the following main steps of the collective data mining approach:

1. Select an appropriate orthonormal representation for the type of data model to be generated.
2. Generate at each site approximate orthonormal basis coefficients.
3. If the global function includes nonlinear terms, move a sample of data sets from each site to a central site and generate there the approximate basis coefficients corresponding to such nonlinear terms.
4. Combine the local models to generate the global model and transform it into the user described model representation.

### 1.2.4.3 Ensemble Learning

Ensemble learning aims at improving classification accuracy by aggregating predictions of multiple classifiers (Tan et al., 2006). An ensemble learning method builds a set of base classifiers from training data and performs classification by voting (in the case of classification) or by averaging (in the case of regression) on the predictions made by each classifier. The final result is the ensemble classifier, which very often have higher classification quality than any single classifier that has been used to compose it.

These are the main steps that compose an ensemble learning strategy for data classification:

1. Using a partitioning tool the input data set is split into a training set and a test set.

2. The training set is given in input to *n* classification algorithms that run concurrently on different processing nodes to build *n* independent classification models.
3. Then, a voter tool *V* accesses the *n* models and performs an ensemble classification by assigning to each instance of the test set the class predicted by the majority of the *n* models generated at the previous step.

The identification of optimal ways to combine the base classifiers is a crucial point here. The most adopted approaches are two schemes called *bagging* and *boosting*. *Bagging* (called voting for classification and averaging for regression) combines the predicted classifications (prediction) from multiple models, or from the same type of model for different learning data. *Bagging* is also used to address the inherent instability of results when applying complex models to relatively small data sets. *Boosting* also combines the decisions of different models, like *bagging*, by amalgamating the various outputs into a single prediction, but it derives the individual models in different ways. In *bagging*, the models receive equal weight, whereas in *boosting*, weighting is used to give more influence to the more successful ones.

## 1.3 SUMMARY

Advances and pervasiveness of computers has been the main driving force of the very huge amounts of digital data that are collected and stored in digital repositories today. Those data volumes can be exploited to extract useful information and producing helpful knowledge for science, industry, public services, and in general for humankind. Data scientists define and use algorithms and methods for instructing computers to learn from data. From this scenario was born the data mining field as a discipline that today provides several different techniques and algorithms for the automatic analysis of large data sets. In this chapter, we introduced the main data mining tasks and presented the most important and most used data mining techniques. Each one of them can be used in several application domains to identify patterns, trends, categories, and find particular events.

Since for the analysis of several complex and large data sources sequential data mining algorithms often need to run for a very long time to produce patterns and models, high performance system and concurrent algorithms are used. In fact, a main approach to reduce response time is based on the use of parallel and distributed algorithms and computing systems. High performance computers, such as multiclusters, clouds, and many-core systems, together with distributed and parallel data mining tools and algorithms, can provide effective solutions to analyze big data sets and obtain results in reasonable time. In general, this approach is based on the exploitation of inherent parallelism of most data mining algorithms. For this reason, in the second part of this chapter we introduce the main issues and discussed some scalable data mining solutions. All the concepts introduced in this chapter, together with those discussed in Chapter 2 pave the way for studying the rest of the book where cloud-based data mining systems, tools, and applications are discussed.

## REFERENCES

Agrawal, R., Shafer, J.C., 1996. Parallel mining of association rules. IEEE Trans. Knowledge Data Eng. 8, 962–969.

Agrawal, R., Srikant, R., 1994. Fast algorithms for mining association rules. In: Proceedings of the 20th VLDB Conference, pp. 487–499.

Agrawal, R., Imielinski, T., Swami, A.N., 1993. Database mining: a performance perspective. IEEE Trans. Knowledge Data Eng. 5 (6), 914–925.

Bruynooghe, M., 1989. Parallel implementation of fast clustering algorithms. In: Proceedings of the International Symposium on High Performance Computing, Elsevier Science, pp. 65–78.

Dempster, A.P., Laird, N.M., Rubin, D.B., 1977. Maximum likelihood from incomplete data via the EM algorithm. J. R. Stat. Soc. B 39 (1), 1–38.

Everitt, B., 1977. Cluster Analysis. Heinemann Educational Books Ltd, London.

Fix, E., Hodges Jr, J.L., 1951. Discriminatory Analysis, non-Parametric Discrimination, USAF School of Aviation Medicine, Randolph Field, Tex., Project 21-49-004, Rept. 4, Contract AF41(128)-31, February 1951.

Foti, D., Lipari, D., Pizzuti, C., Talia, D., 2000. Scalable parallel clustering for data mining on multicomputers. In: Proceedings of the Third International Workshop on High Performance Data Mining, LNCS 1800, Springer-Verlag, pp. 390–398.

Friedman, H.P., Rubin, J., 1967. On some invariant criteria for grouping data. J. Am. Stat. Assoc. 62, 1159–1178.

Han, E.H., Karypis, G., Kumar, V., 2000. Scalable parallel data mining for association rules. IEEE Trans. Knowledge Data Eng. 12 (2), 337–352.

Kargupta, H., Park, B., Hershberger, D., Johnson, E., 2000. A new perspective toward distributed data mining. Advances in Distributed and Parallel Knowledge Discovery. AAAI/MIT Press, Menlo Park, CA.

Kaufman, L., Rousseeuw, P.J., 1990. Finding Groups in Data: An Introduction to Cluster Analysis. John Wiley & Sons, Hoboken, NJ.

Kufrin, R., 1997. Generating C4.5 production rules in parallel. In: Proceedings of the Fourteenth National Conference on Artificial Intelligence, AAAI Press.

Lloyd, S. P., 1982. Least squares quantization in PCM. Unpublished Bell Lab. Tech. Note, portions presented at the Institute of Mathematical Statistics Meeting Atlantic City, NJ, September 1957. Also, IEEE Trans. Information Theory (Special Issue on Quantization), IT-28, pp. 129–137, March 1982.

McQueen, J., 1967. Some methods for classification and analysis of mutivariate observations. In: Proceedings Fifth Berkeley Symposium on Mathematics, Statistics and Probability, vol.1, pp. 281–296.

Olson, C.F., 1995. Parallel algorithms for hierarchical clustering. Parallel Comput. 21, 1313–1325.

Pearson, R.A., 1994. A coarse-grained parallel induction heuristic. In: Kitano, H., Kumar, V., Suttner, C.B. (Eds.), Parallel Processing for Artificial Intelligence 2. Elsevier Science, Amsterdam.

Pizzuti, C., Talia, D., 2003. P-AutoClass: scalable parallel clustering for mining large data sets. IEEE Trans. Knowledge Data Eng. 15 (3), 629–641.

Prodromidis, A.L., Chan, P.K., Stolfo, S.J., 2000. Meta-learning in distributed data mining systems: issues and approaches. Advances in Distributed and Parallel Knowledge Discovery. AAAI/MIT Press, Menlo Park, CA.

Quinlan, J.R., 1986. Induction of Decision trees. Machine Learning 1 (1), 81–106.

Quinlan, J. R., 1987. Generating production rules from decision trees. In: Proceedings International Conference on Artificial Intelligence, Milano, pp. 304–307.

Quinlan, J.R., 1993. C4.5: Programs for Machine Learning. Morgan Kaufmann Publishers, San Mateo, CA.

Shafer, J., Agrawal, R., Mehta, M., 1996. SPRINT: a scalable parallel classifier for data mining. Proceedings of the Twenty-Second International Conference on Very Large Databases.

Talia, D., 2002. Parallelism in knowledge discovery techniques. In: Proceedings Conference PARA 2002, LNCS 2367, Springer-Verlag, pp. 127–136.

Tan, P.N., Steinbach, M., Kumar, V., 2006. Introduction to Data Mining. Addison-Wesley, Boston, MA.

Titterington, D.M., Smith, A.F.M., Makov, U.E., 1985. Statistical Analysis of Finite Mixture Distribution. John Wiley & Sons, New York.

Wu, X., et al., 2008. Top 10 algorithms in data mining. Knowledge Inform. Syst. 14, 1–37.

Zaki, M.J., 1999. Parallel and distributed association mining: a survey. IEEE Concurrency 7 (4), 14–25.

Zaki, M.J., 2000. Scalable algorithms for association mining. IEEE Trans. Knowledge Data Eng. 12 (3), 372–390.

# CHAPTER 2

# Introduction to Cloud Computing

This chapter introduces the basic concepts of cloud computing, which provides scalable storage and processing services that can be used for extracting knowledge from big data repositories. Section 2.1 defines cloud computing and discusses the main service and deployment models adopted by cloud providers. The section also describes some cloud platforms that can be used to implement applications and frameworks for distributed data analysis. Section 2.2 discusses more specifically how cloud computing technologies can be used to implement distributed data analysis systems. The section identifies the main requirements that should be satisfied by a distributed data analysis system, and then discusses how a cloud platform can be used to fulfill such requirements.

## 2.1 CLOUD COMPUTING: DEFINITION, MODELS, AND ARCHITECTURES

As discussed in the previous chapter, an effective solution to extract useful knowledge from big data repositories in reasonable time is exploiting parallel and distributed data mining techniques. It is also necessary and helpful to work with data analysis environments allowing the effective and efficient access, management and mining of such repositories. For example, a scientist can use a data analysis environment to run complex data mining algorithms, validate models, and compare and share results with colleagues located worldwide.

In the past few years, clouds have emerged as effective computing platforms to face the challenge of extracting knowledge from big data repositories, as well as to provide effective and efficient data analysis environments to both researchers and companies. From a client perspective, the cloud is an abstraction for remote, infinitely scalable provisioning of computation and storage resources. From an implementation point of view, cloud systems are based on large sets of computing resources, located somewhere "in the cloud", which are allocated to applications on demand (Barga et al., 2011).

Thus, cloud computing can be defined as a distributed computing paradigm in which all the resources, dynamically scalable and often virtualized, are provided as services over the Internet. Virtualization is a software-based technique that implements the separation of physical computing infrastructures and allows creating various "virtual" computing resources on the same hardware. It is a basic technology that powers cloud computing by making possible to concurrently run different operating environments and multiple applications on the same server. Differently from other distributed computing paradigms, cloud users are not required to have knowledge of, expertise in, or control over the technology infrastructure in the "cloud" that supports them. A number of features define cloud applications, services, data, and infrastructure:

- *Remotely hosted*: Services and/or data are hosted on remote infrastructure.
- *Ubiquitous*: Services or data are available from anywhere.
- *Pay-per-use*: The result is a utility computing model similar to that of traditional utilities, like gas and electricity, where you pay for what you use.

We can also use the popular National Institute of Standards and Technology (NIST) definition of cloud computing to highlight its main features (Mell and Grance, 2011): "Cloud computing is a model for enabling convenient, on-demand network access to a shared pool of configurable computing resources (e.g., networks, servers, storage, applications, and services) that can be rapidly provisioned and released with minimal management effort or service provider interaction". From the NIST definition, we can identify five essential characteristics of cloud computing systems, which are on-demand self-service, broad network access, resource pooling, rapid elasticity, and measured service.

Cloud systems can be classified on the basis of their *service model* (Software as a Service, Platform as a Service, Infrastructure as a Service) and their *deployment model* (public cloud, private cloud, hybrid cloud).

## 2.1.1 Service Models

Cloud computing vendors provide their services according to three main models: Software as a Service (SaaS), Platform as a Service (PaaS), and Infrastructure as a Service (IaaS).

*Software as a Service* defines a delivery model in which software and data are provided through Internet to customers as ready-to-use services. Specifically, software and associated data are hosted by providers, and customers access them without need to use any additional hardware or software. Moreover, customers normally pay a monthly/yearly fee, with no additional purchase of infrastructure or software licenses. Examples of common SaaS applications are Webmail systems (e.g., Gmail), calendars (Yahoo Calendar), document management (Microsoft Office 365), image manipulation (Photoshop Express), customer relationship management (Salesforce), and others.

In *Platform as a Service* model, cloud vendors deliver a computing platform typically including databases, application servers, development environment for building, testing, and running custom applications. Developers can just focus on deploying of applications since cloud providers are in charge of maintenance and optimization of the environment and underlying infrastructure. Hence, customers are helped in application development as they use a set of "environment" services that are modular and can be easily integrated. Normally, the applications are developed as ready-to-use SaaS. Google App Engine, Microsoft Azure, Salesforce.com are some examples of PaaS cloud environments.

Finally, *Infrastructure as a Service* is an outsourcing model under which customers rent resources like CPUs, disks, or more complex resources like virtualized servers or operating systems to support their operations (e.g., Amazon EC2, RackSpace Cloud). Users of an IaaS have normally skills on system and network administration, as they must deal with configuration, operation, and maintenance tasks. Compared to the PaaS approach, the IaaS model has a higher system administration costs for the user; on the other hand, IaaS allows a full customization of the execution environment. Developers can scale up or down its services adding or removing virtual machines, easily instantiable from virtual machine images.

Table 2.1 describes how the three service models satisfy the requirements of developers and final users, in terms of flexibility, scalability, portability, security, maintenance, and costs.

## 2.1.2 Deployment Models

Cloud computing services are delivered according to three main deployment models: public, private, or hybrid.

**Table 2.1  How SaaS, PaaS, and IaaS Satisfy the Requirements of Developers and Final Users**

| Requirements | SaaS | PaaS | IaaS |
|---|---|---|---|
| Flexibility | Users can customize the application interface and control its behavior, but cannot decide which software and hardware components are used to support its execution. | Developers write, customize, test their application using libraries and supporting tools compatible with the platform. Users can choose what kind of virtual storage and compute resources are used for executing their application. | Developers have to build the servers that will host their applications, and configure operating system and software modules on top of such servers. |
| Scalability | The underlying computing and storage resources normally scale automatically to match application demand, so that users do not have to allocate resources manually. The result depends only on the level of elasticity provided by the cloud system. | Like the SaaS model, the underlying computing and storage resources normally scale automatically. | Developers can use new storage and compute resources, but their applications must be scalable and allow the dynamic inclusion of new resources. |
| Portability | There can be problems to move applications to other providers, since some software and tools could not work on different systems. For example, application data may be in a format that cannot be read by another provider. | Applications can be moved to another provider only if the new provider shares with the old one the required platform tools and services. | If a provider allows to download a virtual machine in a standard format, it may be moved to a different provider. |
| Security | Users can control only some security settings of their applications (e.g., using https instead of http to access some Web pages). Additional security layers (e.g., data replication) are hidden to the user and managed directly by the system. | The security of code and additional libraries used to build application is responsibility of the developer. | Developers must take care of security issues from operating system to application layer. |
| Maintenance | Users have not to carry maintenance tasks. | Developers are in charge of maintaining only their application; other software components and the hardware are maintained by the provider. | Developers are in charge of all software components, including the operating system; hardware is maintained by the provider. |
| Cost | Users typically pay a monthly/yearly fee for using the software, with no additional fee for the infrastructure. | Developers pay for the compute and storage resources, and for the licenses of libraries and tools used by their applications. | Developers pay for all the software and hardware resources used. |

A *public cloud* provider delivers services to the general public through the Internet. The users of a public cloud have little or no control over the underlying technology infrastructure. In this model, services can be offered for free, or provided according to a pay-per-use policy. The main public providers, such as Google, Microsoft, Amazon, own and manage their proprietary data centers delivering services built on top of them.

A *private cloud* provider offers operations and functionalities "as a service", which are deployed over a company intranet or hosted in a remote data center. Often, small and medium-sized IT companies prefer this deployment model as it offers advanced security and data control solutions that are not available in the public cloud model.

Finally, a *hybrid cloud* is the composition of two or more (private or public) clouds that remain different entities but are linked together. Companies can extend their private clouds using other private clouds from partner companies, or public clouds. In particular, by extending the private infrastructure with public cloud resources, it is possible to satisfy peaks of requests, better serve user requests, and implement high-availability strategies.

Figure 2.1 depicts the general architecture of a public cloud and its main components, as outlined in (Li et al., 2010). Users access

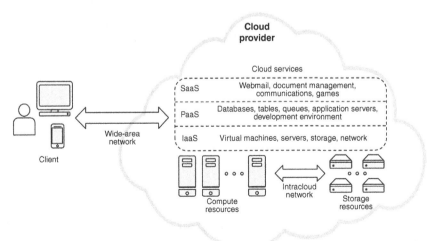

*Fig. 2.1. General architecture of a public cloud.*

cloud computing services using *client* devices, such as desktop computers, laptops, tablets, and smartphones. Through these devices, users access and interact with cloud-based services using a Web browser or desktop/mobile app. The business software and user's data are executed and stored on servers hosted in cloud data centers that provide *storage and compute resources*. Resources include thousands of servers and storage devices connected to each other through an *intracloud network*. The transfer of data between data center and users takes place on *wide-area network*.

Several technologies and standards are used by the different components of the architecture. For example, users can interact with cloud services through SOAP-based or RESTful Web services (Richardson and Ruby, 2007). *HTML5* and *Ajax* technologies allow Web interfaces to cloud services to have the look and interactivity equivalent to those of desktop applications. *Open Cloud Computing Interface* (OCCI)[1] specifies how cloud providers can deliver their compute, data, and network resources through a standardized interface. Another example is *Open Virtualization Format* (OVF)[2] for packaging and distributing virtual devices or software (e.g., virtual operating systems) to be run on virtual machines.

### 2.1.3 Cloud Environments

This section introduces four representative examples of cloud environments: *Microsoft Azure* as an example of public PaaS, *Amazon Web Services* as the most popular public IaaS, *OpenNebula* and *OpenStack* as examples of private IaaS. These environments can be used to implement applications and frameworks for data analysis in the cloud.

#### 2.1.3.1 Microsoft Azure

Azure[3] is an environment and a set of cloud services that can be used to develop cloud-oriented applications, or to enhance existing applications with cloud-based capabilities. The platform provides on-demand compute and storage resources exploiting the computational and storage power of the Microsoft data centers. Azure is designed for supporting

---

[1]OCCI Working Group, http://www.occi-wg.org

[2]OVF Specification, http://www.dmtf.org/sites/default/files/standards/documents/DSP 0243_1.1.0.pdf

[3] Microsoft Azure, http://www.microsoft.com/azure

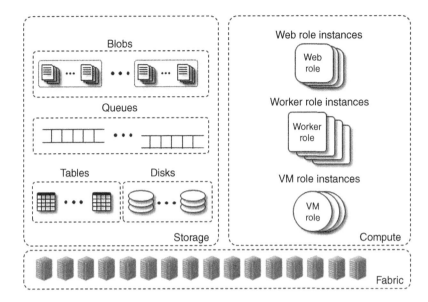

*Fig. 2.2. Microsoft Azure.*

high availability and dynamic scaling services that match user needs with a pay-per-use pricing model.

The Azure platform can be used to perform the storage of large datasets, execute large volumes of batch computations, and develop SaaS applications targeted towards end-users.

Microsoft Azure includes three basic components/services as shown in Figure 2.2:

- *Compute*: is the computational environment to execute cloud applications. Each application is structured into roles: *Web role*, for Web-based applications; *Worker role*, for batch applications; *VM role*, for virtual-machine images.
- *Storage*: provides scalable storage to manage binary and text data (*Blobs*), nonrelational tables (*Tables*), queues for asynchronous communication between components (*Queues*), and virtual disks (*Disks*).
- *Fabric controller*: whose aim is to build a network of interconnected nodes from the physical machines of a single data center. The Compute and Storage services are built on top of this component.

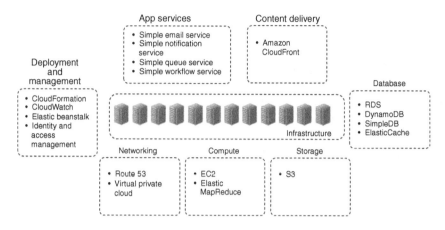

*Fig. 2.3. Amazon Web Services.*

Microsoft Azure provides standard interfaces that allow developers to interact with its services. Moreover, developers can use IDEs like Microsoft Visual Studio and Eclipse to easily design and publish Azure applications.

### 2.1.3.2  Amazon Web Services

Amazon offers compute and storage resources of its IT infrastructure to developers in the form of Web services. Amazon Web Services (AWS)[4] is a large set of cloud services that can be composed by users to build their SaaS applications or integrate traditional software with cloud capabilities (see Figure 2.3). It is simple to interact with these service since Amazon provides SDKs for the main programming languages and platforms (e.g., Java, .Net, PHP, Android).

AWS includes the following main services:

- Compute: *Elastic Compute Cloud* (EC2) allows creating and running virtual servers; *Amazon Elastic MapReduce* for building and executing MapReduce applications.
- Storage: *Simple Storage Service* (S3), which allows storing and retrieving data via the Internet.
- Database: *Relational Database Service* (RDS) for relational tables; *DynamoDB* for nonrelational tables; *SimpleDB* for managing small datasets; *ElasticCache* for caching data.

---

[4]Amazon Web Services, http://aws.amazon.com/

- Networking: *Route 53*, a DNS Web service; *Virtual Private Cloud* for implementing a virtual network.
- Deployment and Management: *CloudFormation* for creating a collection of ready-to-use virtual machines with preinstalled software (e.g., Web applications); *CloudWatch* for monitoring AWS resources; *Elastic Beanstalk* to deploy and execute custom applications written in Java, PHP and other languages; *Identity and Access Management* to securely control access to AWS services and resources.
- Content delivery: *Amazon CloudFront* makes easy to distribute content via a global network of edge locations.
- App services: *Simple Email Service* providing a basic email-sending service; *Simple Notification Service* to notify users; *Simple Queue Service* that implements a message queue; *Simple Workflow Service* to implement workflow-based applications.

Even though Amazon is best known to be the first IaaS provider (based on its EC2 and S3 services), it is now also a PaaS provider, with services like Elastic Beanstalk.

### 2.1.3.3 OpenNebula

OpenNebula (Sotomayor et al., 2009) is an open-source framework mainly used to build private and hybrid clouds. The main component of the OpenNebula architecture (see Figure 2.4) is the *Core*, which creates

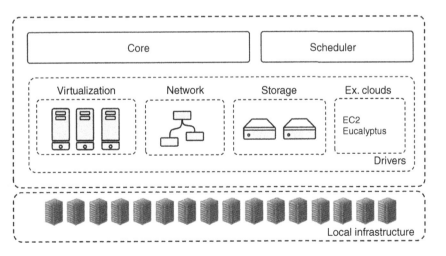

*Fig. 2.4.  OpenNebula.*

and controls virtual machines by interconnecting them with a virtual network environment. Moreover, the Core interacts with specific storage, network, and virtualization operations through pluggable components called *Drivers*. In this way, OpenNebula is independent from the underlying infrastructure and offers a uniform management environment.

The Core also supports the deployment of *Services*, which are a set of linked components (e.g., Web server, database) executed on several virtual machines. Another component is the *Scheduler*, which is responsible for allocating the virtual machines on the physical servers. To this end, the Scheduler interacts with the Core component through appropriate deployment commands.

OpenNebula can implement a hybrid cloud using specific Drivers that allow to interact with external clouds. In this way, the local infrastructure can be supplemented with computing and storage resources from public clouds. Currently, OpenNebula includes drivers for using resources from Amazon EC2 and Eucalyptus (Nurmi et al., 2009), another open source cloud framework.

### 2.1.3.4 OpenStack

OpenStack[5] is a cloud operating system that allows the management of large pools of processing, storage, and networking resources in a datacenter through a Web-based interface. The system has been designed, developed and released following four open principles:

- *Open source*: OpenStack is released under the terms of the Apache License 2.0;
- *Open design*: Every six months there is a design summit to gather requirements and define new specifications for the upcoming release;
- *Open development*: A publicly available source code repository is maintained for the entire development process;
- *Open Community*: Most decisions are made by the OpenStack community using a lazy consensus model.

The modular architecture of OpenStack is composed by four main components, as shown in Figure 2.5.

---

[5]OpenStack, http://www.openstack.org/

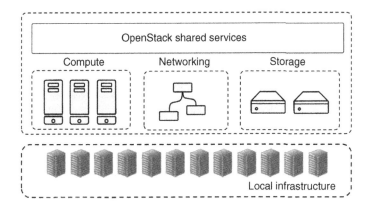

*Fig. 2.5. OpenStack.*

OpenStack *Compute* provides virtual servers upon demand by managing the pool of processing resources available in the datacenter. It supports different virtualization technologies (e.g., VMware, KVM) and is designed to scale horizontally. OpenStack *Storage* provides a scalable and redundant storage system. It supports Object Storage and Block Storage: the former allows storing and retrieving objects and files in the datacenter; the latter allows creating, attaching and detaching of block devices to servers. OpenStack *Networking* manages the networks and IP addresses. Finally, OpenStack *Shared Services* are additional services provided to ease the use of the datacenter. For instance, Identity Service maps users and services, Image Service manages server images, Database Service provides a relational database.

## 2.2 CLOUD COMPUTING SYSTEMS FOR DATA-INTENSIVE APPLICATIONS

Cloud systems can be effectively exploited to support data-intensive applications since they provide scalable storage and processing services, as well as software platforms for developing and running data analysis environments on top of such services. This section discusses how cloud computing technologies can be exploited to implement distributed data analysis systems for data-intensive KDD applications. We start identifying the main *functional* and *nonfunctional* requirements that should be satisfied by a distributed data analysis system for KDD applications.

Functional requirements specify which functionalities the system should provide; nonfunctional requirements refer to quality criteria mostly related to system performance.

## 2.2.1 Functional Requirements

The functional requirements that should be satisfied by a distributed data analysis system can be grouped into two main classes: *resource management* and *application management* requirements. The former refers to requirements related to the management of all the resources (data, tools, results) that may be involved in a KDD application; the latter refers to requirements related to the design and execution of the applications themselves.

### 2.2.1.1 Resource Management

Resources of interests in distributed KDD applications include *data sources*, *knowledge discovery tools*, and *knowledge discovery results*. Therefore, a distributed data analysis system should deal with the following resource management requirements:

- *Data management*: Data sources can be in different formats, such as relational databases, plain files, or semistructured documents (e.g., XML files). The system should provide mechanisms to store and access such data sources independently from their specific format. In addition, metadata formalisms should be defined and used to describe the relevant information associated with data sources (e.g., location, format, availability, available views), in order to enable their effective access and manipulation.
- *Tool management*: Knowledge discovery tools include algorithms and services for data selection, preprocessing, transformation, data mining, and results evaluation. The system should provide mechanisms to access and use such tools independently from their specific implementation. Metadata have to be used to describe the most important features of KDD tools (e.g., their function, location, usage).
- *Result management*: The knowledge obtained as the result of a knowledge discovery process is represented by a knowledge (or data mining) model. The system should provide mechanisms to store and access such models, independently from their structure and format. As for data and tools, data mining models need to be described by metadata to explain and interpret their content, and to enable their effective retrieval.

## 2.2.1.2  Application Management

A distributed data analysis system must provide effective mechanisms to design data-intensive KDD applications (*design management*) and control their execution (*execution management*):

- *Design management*: Distributed data analysis applications range from simple data mining tasks, to complex data mining patterns expressed as workflows. From a design perspective, three main classes of knowledge discovery applications can be identified: *single-task applications*, in which a single data mining task such as classification, clustering, or association rules discovery is performed on a given data source; *parameter sweeping applications*, in which a dataset is analyzed using multiple instances of the same data mining algorithm with different parameters; *workflow-based applications*, in which possibly complex knowledge discovery applications are specified as graphs that link together data sources, data mining algorithms, and visualization tools. A general system should provide environments to effectively design all the above-mentioned classes of data analysis applications.

- *Execution management*: The system has to provide a distributed execution environment that supports the efficient execution of data analysis applications designed by users. Since applications range from single tasks to complex knowledge discovery workflows, the execution environment should cope with such a variety of applications. In particular, the execution environment should provide the following functionalities, which are related to the different phases of application execution: accessing the data sources to be mined; allocating the needed compute resources; running the application based on the user specifications, which may be expressed as a workflow; presenting the results to the user. Additionally, the system should allow users to monitor the application execution.

## 2.2.2  Nonfunctional Requirements

Nonfunctional requirements can be defined at three levels: *user*, *architecture*, and *infrastructure*. User requirements specify how the user should interact with the system; architecture requirements specify which principles should inspire the design of the system architecture; finally, infrastructure requirements describe the nonfunctional features of the underlying computational infrastructure.

#### 2.2.2.1 User Requirements

From a user point of view, the following nonfunctional requirements should be satisfied:

- *Usability*: The system should be easy to use by the end-users, without the need of undertaking any specialized training.
- *Ubiquitous access*: Users should be able to access the system from anywhere using standard network technologies (e.g., Web sites) either from a desktop PC or from a mobile device.
- *Data protection*: Data represents a key asset for users; therefore, the system should protect data to be mined and inferred knowledge from both unauthorized access and intentional/incidental losses.

#### 2.2.2.2 Architecture Requirements

The main nonfunctional requirements at the architectural level are:

- *Service-orientation*: The architecture should be designed as a set of network-enabled software components (services) implementing the different operational capabilities of the system, to enable their effective reuse, composition, and interoperability.
- *Openness and extensibility*: The architecture should be open to the integration of new knowledge discovery tools and services. Moreover, existing services should be open for extension, but closed for modification, according to the open-closed principle.
- *Independence from infrastructure*: The architecture should be designed to be as independent as possible from the underlying infrastructure; in other terms, the system services should be able to exploit the basic functionalities provided by different infrastructures.

#### 2.2.2.3 Infrastructure Requirements

Finally, from the infrastructure perspective, the following nonfunctional requirements should be satisfied:

- *Standardized access*: The infrastructure should expose its services using standard technologies (e.g., Web services), to make them usable as building blocks for high-level services or applications.
- *Heterogeneous/Distributed data support*: The infrastructure should be able to cope with very large and high dimensional datasets, stored in different formats in a single data center, or geographically distributed across many sites.

- *Availability*: The infrastructure should be in a functioning condition even in the presence of failures that affect a subset of the hardware/ software resources. Thus, effective mechanisms (e.g., redundancy) should be implemented to ensure dependable access to sensitive resources such as user data and applications.

- *Scalability*: The infrastructure should be able to handle a growing workload (deriving from larger data to process or heavier algorithms to execute) in an efficient and effective way, by dynamically allocating the needed resources (processors, storage, network). Moreover, as soon as the workload decreases, the infrastructure should release the unneeded resources.

- *Efficiency*: The infrastructure should minimize resource consumption for a given task to execute. In the case of parallel/distributed tasks, efficient allocation of processing nodes should be guaranteed. Additionally, the infrastructure should be highly utilized so to provide efficient services.

- *Security*: The infrastructure should provide effective security mechanisms to ensure data protection, identity management, and privacy.

## 2.2.3  Cloud Models for Distributed Data Analysis

As discussed in Section 2.1.1, cloud providers classify their services into three main categories: Software as a Service (SaaS), where each software or application executed is provided through Internet to customers as ready-to-use services; *Platform as a Service* (PaaS), providing platform services such as databases, application servers, or environments for building, testing and running custom applications; *Infrastructure as a Service* (IaaS), providing computing resources like CPUs, memory, and storage, for running virtualized systems over the cloud.

Data analysis services for data-intensive KDD applications may be implemented within each of the three categories listed above:

- *KDD as SaaS*: where a single well-defined data mining algorithm or a ready-to-use knowledge discovery tool is provided as an Internet service to end-users, who may directly use it through a Web browser.

- *KDD as PaaS*: where a supporting platform is provided to developers that have to build their own applications or extend existing ones. Developers can just focus on the definition of their KDD applications without worrying about the underlying infrastructure or distributed computation issues.

- *KDD as IaaS*: where a set of virtualized resources are provided to developers as a computing infrastructure to run their data mining applications or to implement their KDD systems from scratch.

In all three scenarios listed above, the cloud plays the role of infrastructure provider, even if at the SaaS and PaaS layers the infrastructure can be transparent to the end-user.

As an example of PaaS approach, Table 2.2 summarizes how the Microsoft Azure components and mechanisms, introduced in Section 2.1.3.1, can be effectively exploited to fulfill the functional requirements of a distributed data analysis system that have been introduced in Section 2.2.1.

**Table 2.2  Using Microsoft Azure to Fulfill the Functional Requirements of a Distributed Data Analysis System**

| Functional Requirements | | Microsoft Azure Components |
|---|---|---|
| Resource management | Data | *Different data formats*: Binary large objects (Blobs); nonrelational tables (Tables); queues for communication data (Queues); relational databases (SQL Database).<br>*Metadata support*: Tables/SQL Databases to store data descriptions; custom description fields can be added to Blobs containing data sources. |
| | Tools | *Implementation-independent access*: Tools can be exposed as Web services.<br>*Metadata support*: Tables/SQL Databases to store tools descriptions; custom description fields can be added to Blobs containing binary tools; WSDL descriptions for Web services. |
| | Results | *Models storing*: Blobs to store results either in textual or visual form.<br>*Metadata support*: Tables/SQL Databases to describe models format; custom description fields can be added to Blobs containing data mining models. |
| Application management | Design | *Single-task applications*: Programming the execution of a single Web service or binary tool on a single Worker role instance.<br>*Parameter sweeping applications*: Programming the concurrent execution of a set of Web services or binary tools on a set of Worker role instances.<br>*Workflow-based applications*: Programming the coordinated execution of a set of Web services or binary tools on a set of Worker role instances. |
| | Execution | *Storage resources access*: Managed by the Storage layer.<br>*Compute resources allocation*: Managed by the Compute layer.<br>*Application execution and monitoring*: Web services/Worker role instances to run single tasks; Tables to store tasks information; Web role instance to present monitoring information.<br>*Results presentation*: Blobs/Tables to store/interpret the inferred models; Web role instance to present results. |

## 2.3 SUMMARY

Clouds provide scalable storage and processing services that can be used for extracting knowledge from big data repositories, as well as software platforms for developing and running data analysis environments on top of such services. In this chapter we provided an overview of cloud technologies by describing the main service models (Software as a Service, Platform as a Service, and Infrastructure as a Service) and deployment models (public, private, or hybrid clouds) adopted by cloud providers. We also described representative examples of cloud environments (Microsoft Azure, Amazon Web Services, OpenNebula, and OpenStack) that can be used to implement applications and frameworks for data analysis in the cloud. Finally, after having identified the main requirements that should be satisfied by a distributed data analysis system, we discussed as an example how the Microsoft Azure components and mechanisms can be used to fulfill such requirements.

## REFERENCES

Barga, R., Gannon, D., Reed, D., 2011. The client and the cloud: democratizing research computing. IEEE Internet Comput. 15 (1), 72–75.

Li, A., Yang, X., Kandula, S., Zhang, M., 2010. CloudCmp: comparing public cloud providers. Tenth ACM SIGCOMM Conference on Internet Measurement (IMC'10), New York, USA.

Mell, P., Grance, T., 2011. The NIST Definition of Cloud Computing. NIST Special Publication 800-145.

Nurmi, D., Wolski, R., Grzegorczyk, C., Obertelli, G., Soman, S., Youseff, L., Zagorodnov, D., 2009. The eucalyptus open-source cloud computing system. In: Proceedings of the Ninth IEEE/ACM International Symposium on Cluster Computing and the Grid (CCGRID'09), Washington, USA.

Richardson, L., Ruby, S., 2007. RESTful Web Services. O'Reilly & Associates, California.

Sotomayor, B., Montero, R.S., Llorente, I.M., Foster, I., 2009. Virtual infrastructure management in private and hybrid clouds. IEEE Internet Comput. 13, 14–22.

# CHAPTER 3

# Models and Techniques for Cloud-Based Data Analysis

This chapter discusses the main models and techniques used for designing cloud-based data analysis applications. The models presented here are based on MapReduce, workflows, and NoSQL database management systems. In the next sections, we explain how these three main approaches offer scalability for mining Big Data repositories on clouds. Section 3.1 introduces the MapReduce model and how it can be used to implement scalable data analysis algorithms and applications. Section 3.2 discusses the workflow systems, presents some workflow management systems (WMSs) implemented on cloud architectures and discusses their main features to implement data analysis applications. Finally, Section 3.3 describes NoSQL database systems that were recently developed to efficiently manage large volumes of data. In several application cases NoSQL databases are more scalable and provide higher performance than relational databases. Here we describe some representative NoSQL systems, and discuss use cases for NoSQL databases with a focus on data analytics.

## 3.1 MapReduce FOR DATA ANALYSIS

MapReduce is a system and method for efficient large-scale data processing proposed by Google in 2004 (Dean and Ghemawat, 2004) to cope with the challenge of processing very large input data generated by Internet-based applications. Since its introduction, MapReduce has proven to be applicable in a wide range of domains, including machine learning and data mining, social data analysis, financial analysis, scientific simulation, image retrieval and processing, blog crawling, machine translation, language modeling, and bioinformatics. Today, MapReduce is widely recognized as one of the most important programming models for cloud computing environments, as it is supported by Google and other leading cloud providers such as Amazon, with its Elastic MapReduce service,[1] and Microsoft, with its HDInsight,[2] and used on top of private cloud infrastructures such as OpenNebula, with its Sahara service.[3]

The MapReduce abstraction is inspired by the *map* and *reduce* primitives designed in Lisp and other functional languages. A user defines a MapReduce application in terms of a *map* function that processes a (*key, value*) pair, to generate a list of intermediate (*key, value*) pairs, and a *reduce* function that merges all intermediate values associated with the same intermediate key. Current MapReduce implementations, like Hadoop (White, 2009), are based on a master–slave architecture. A user node submits a job to a master node, which selects idle workers and assigns a map or reduce task to each one. When all the tasks are complete, the master node returns the result to the user node.

For years, grid and distributed computing systems have been widely used for data processing. These systems work well with compute-intensive jobs, but require a lot of network bandwidth to handle huge amounts of distributed data. To reduce the network bandwidth bottleneck, which often affects distributed data analysis systems, MapReduce implements a data locality feature, so that the computation tasks are located near the input data (e.g., same node, same rack) to optimize performance and save energy (Zhenhua Guo et al., 2012). In contrast to RDBMS, that is ideal for storing and processing structured data, MapReduce can be used to process semistructured or unstructured data in parallel, since data is evaluated at processing time. Moreover, MapReduce is designed to process very large amounts of data using hundreds or thousands of machines in distributed/parallel environments, so the model must tolerate machine failures. The failure of a worker is managed by re-executing its task on another worker. An optimization related to failure handling provided by MapReduce frameworks is the scheduling of redundant execution of tasks near the end of the job for reducing its completion time in case of machine failures and data loss.

Thanks to the features described above, MapReduce is widely used to implement scalable data analysis algorithms and applications executed on multiple machines to efficiently analyze big amounts of data.

---

## 3.1.1  MapReduce Paradigm

This section briefly describes various operations that are performed by a generic application to transform input data into output data according to the MapReduce model.

Users must define a *map* and a *reduce* function (Dean and Ghemawat, 2008). The *map* function processes a (*key, value*) pair and returns a list of intermediate (*key, value*) pairs:

$$map(k1, v1) \rightarrow \text{list}(k2, v2)$$

The *reduce* function merges all intermediate values having the same intermediate key:

$$reduce(k2, \text{list}(v2)) \rightarrow \text{list}(v3)$$

As an example, let us consider the creation of an inverted index for a large set of Web documents. In its basic form, an inverted index contains a set of words (index terms), and for each word it specifies the IDs of all the documents that contain that word. Using a MapReduce approach, the *map* function parses each document and emits a sequence of (word, documentID) pairs. The *reduce* function takes all pairs for a given word, sorts the corresponding document IDs, and emits a (word, list(documentID)) pair. The set of all output pairs generated by the reduce function forms the inverted index for the input documents.

In general, the whole transformation process performed in a MapReduce application can be described through the following steps (Figure 3.1):

1. A master process receives a job descriptor, which specifies the MapReduce job to be executed. The job descriptor contains, among other information, the location of the input data, which may be accessed using a distributed file system.
2. According to the job descriptor, the master starts a number of mapper and reducer processes on different machines. At the same time, it starts a process that reads the input data from its location, partitions that data into a set of splits, and distributes those splits into various mappers.
3. After receiving its data partition, each mapper process executes the *map* function (provided as part of the job descriptor) to generate a

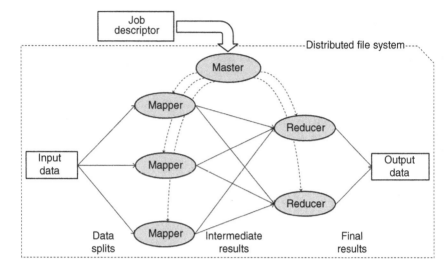

Fig. 3.1.  Execution phases of a generic MapReduce application.

list of intermediate key/value pairs. Then these pairs are grouped on the basis of their keys.

4. All pairs with the same keys are assigned to the same reducer process. Hence, each reducer process executes the *reduce* function (defined by the job descriptor), which merges all the values associated with the same key to generate a possibly smaller set of values.

5. Then results generated by each reducer process is collected and delivered to a location specified by the job descriptor, so as to form the final output data.

Distributed file systems are the most popular solutions for accessing input/output data in MapReduce systems, particularly in standard computing environments like a data center or a cluster of computers.

To define complex applications that cannot be coded with a single MapReduce job, users need to compose chains or, in a more general way, workflows of MapReduce jobs. Chains can be easily implemented with the output of a job that goes to a distributed file system and is used as an input for the next job. Figure 3.2 shows an example of MapReduce chain, in which some data sources are analyzed sequentially by three MapReduce jobs, to produce the final output.

*Fig. 3.2.  Example of MapReduce chain.*

### 3.1.2 MapReduce Frameworks

Hadoop is the best-known MapReduce implementation and it is commonly used to develop parallel applications analyzing big amounts of data. Hadoop can be adopted for developing distributed and parallel applications using many programming languages (e.g., Java, Ruby, Python, C++). It relieves developers from having to deal with classical distributed computing issues, such as load balancing, fault tolerance, data locality, and network bandwidth saving. The Hadoop project is not only about the MapReduce programming model (Hadoop MapReduce module), but also includes other modules such as:

- *Hadoop Distributed File System* (*HDFS*): a distributed file system providing fault tolerance with automatic recovery, portability across heterogeneous commodity hardware and operating systems, high throughput access and data reliability.
- *Hadoop YARN*: a framework for cluster resource management and job scheduling.
- *Hadoop Common*: common utilities that support the other Hadoop modules.

With the introduction of YARN in 2013, Hadoop turns from a batch processing solution into a platform to run a large variety of data applications, such as streaming, in-memory, and graphs analysis. As a result, Hadoop became a reference for several other frameworks, such as Giraph[4] for graph analysis; Storm[5] for streaming data analysis; Hive[6], which is a data warehouse software for querying and managing large datasets; Pig[7], which is as a dataflow language for exploring large datasets; Tez[8] for executing complex directed-acyclic graphs of data

---

[4]http://giraph.apache.org/
[5]http://storm.apache.org
[6]http://hive.apache.org
[7]http://pig.apache.org
[8]http://tez.apache.org/

processing tasks; Oozie[9], which is a workflow scheduler system for managing Hadoop jobs; Spark[10], which is a cluster computing framework for in-memory machine learning and data analysis. In contrast to Hadoop's two-stage MapReduce paradigm, in which intermediate data are always stored in distributed file systems, Spark stores data in cluster's memory and queries it repeatedly so as to obtain better performance for some class of applications (e.g., iterative machine learning algorithms) (Xin et al., 2013).

Besides Hadoop and its ecosystem, several other MapReduce implementations have been implemented within other systems, including GridGain,[11] Skynet,[12] MapSharp,[13] and Twister (Ekanayake et al., 2010). One of the most popular alternatives to Hadoop is Disco,[14] which is a lightweight, open-source framework for distributed computing. The Disco core is written in Erlang, a functional language designed to build fault-tolerant distributed applications. Disco has been used for a variety of purposes, such as log analysis, text indexing, probabilistic modeling, and data mining.

Some other frameworks focused toward adapting the MapReduce model to specific computing environments. Among them, Phoenix (Ranger et al., 2007) is an implementation of MapReduce for shared-memory systems that includes a programming API and a runtime system. It uses threads to spawn parallel map or reduce tasks and shared-memory buffers to facilitate communication without excessive data copying. Overall, Phoenix proves that MapReduce is a useful programming and concurrency management approach also for multicore and multiprocessor systems.

MOON (Lin et al., 2010) is a system designed to support MapReduce jobs in opportunistic environments. It extends Hadoop with adaptive task and data scheduling algorithms to offer reliable MapReduce

---

[9]http://oozie.apache.org/
[10]http://spark.apache.org
[11]http://www.gridgain.com/
[12]http://github.com/skynetservices/skynet
[13]http://mapsharp.codeplex.com
[14]http://discoproject.org/

services on a hybrid resource architecture, where volunteer computing systems are supplemented by a small set of dedicated nodes. The adaptive task and data scheduling algorithms in MOON distinguish different types of MapReduce data and node outages, in order to place tasks and data on volatile and dedicated nodes.

Tang et al. (2010) designed a system to support MapReduce applications in desktop grids. The proposed system exploits the BitDew middleware (Fedak et al., 2009), which is a programmable environment for automatic and transparent data management on desktop grids. BitDew relies on a specific set of metadata to drive key data management operations, namely life cycle, distribution, placement, replication, and fault tolerance with a high level of abstraction.

MISCO (Dou et al., 2010) is a framework for supporting MapReduce applications on mobile systems. Although Misco follows the general design of MapReduce, it differs in two main aspects: task assignment and data transfer. The first aspect is managed with a polling strategy. For data transfer, instead of a distributed file system that is not practical in a mobile scenario, Misco uses HTTP to communicate requests, task information, and transfer data.

Finally, P2P-MapReduce (Marozzo et al., 2012b) is a framework that exploits a peer-to-peer model to manage node churn, master failures, and job recovery in a decentralized but effective way, so as to provide a more reliable MapReduce middleware, which can be effectively exploited in dynamic cloud infrastructures. The P2P-MapReduce framework does not suffer from job failures, even in the presence of very high churn rates, thus enabling the execution of reliable MapReduce applications in dynamic cloud infrastructures.

### 3.1.3 MapReduce Algorithms and Applications

In the last few years, all major data mining algorithms have been re-implemented in MapReduce such as K-means (Ekanayake et al., 2008), Apriori (Lin et al., 2012), C4.5 (Gongqing et al., 2009), and support vector machines (Sun and Fox, 2012). Chu et al. (2007) demonstrated that MapReduce shows a linear speedup with an increasing number of processors in a variety of learning algorithms such as Naive Bayes, neural networks, and Expectation–Maximization probabilistic clustering.

Ricardo project (Das et al., 2010) is a platform that integrates R[15] statistical tools and Hadoop to support parallel data analysis.

Mahout[16] is a machine learning framework that provides scalable machine learning libraries on top of Hadoop. It supplies various algorithms for clustering, classification, and collaborative filtering, which can be run in parallel on a Hadoop cluster. MLlib[17] is a scalable machine learning library on top of Spark. It implements many common machine learning and statistical algorithms to analyze large-scale data hosted in the memory.

As mentioned earlier in this section, MapReduce has proven to be applicable to a wide range of domains, including social data analysis (Tang et al., 2009), financial analysis (Coleman et al., 2012), image retrieval and processing (Cary et al., 2009), trajectory analysis (Ma et al., 2009) and bioinformatics (Ekanayake et al., 2008).

Tang et al. (2009) analyzed a large social network to find out how nodes (users and entities) are influenced by others for various reasons. To address this issue the authors proposed a model, called Topical Affinity Propagation, to describe the topic-level social influence on large networks. Their learning task was performed in a distributed system using MapReduce.

Coleman et al. (2012) showed how numerically intensive tasks for pricing, risk analysis, forecasting, and automated trading can be efficiently dealt through MapReduce algorithms. Cary et al. (2009) showed how MapReduce can be used to analyze spatial data, that is, raster data (satellite/aerial digital images) or vector data (points, lines, polygons), while Ma et al. (2009) show the use of MapReduce for query processing over trajectory data. The use of MapReduce for data intensive scientific analysis and bioinformatics is deeply analyzed in Ekanayake et al. (2008). The authors showed that most scientific data analyses (e.g., SMPD algorithm) can benefit from MapReduce to achieve speedup and scalability.

---

[15]http://www.r-project.org
[16]http://mahout.apache.org
[17]http://spark.apache.org/mllib/

## 3.2 DATA ANALYSIS WORKFLOWS

A workflow consists of a series of activities, events, or tasks that must be performed to accomplish a goal and/or obtain a result. For example, a data analysis workflow can be designed as a sequence of preprocessing, analysis, postprocessing, and interpretation steps. At a practical level, a workflow can be implemented as a computer program, can be expressed in a programming language or paradigm that allows expressing the basic workflow steps, and includes mechanisms to orchestrate them.

Workflows have emerged as an effective paradigm to address the complexity of scientific and business applications. The wide availability of high-performance computing systems, grids and clouds, allowed scientists and engineers to implement more complex applications to access and process large data repositories and run scientific experiments *in silico* on distributed computing platforms. Most of these applications are designed as workflows that include data analysis, scientific computation methods, and complex simulation techniques.

The design and execution of many scientific applications require tools and high-level mechanisms. Simple and complex workflows are often used to reach this goal. For this reason, in the past years, many efforts have been devoted towards the development of distributed WMSs for scientific applications. Workflows provide a declarative way of specifying the high-level logic of an application, hiding the low-level details that are not fundamental for application design. They are also able to integrate existing software modules, datasets, and services in complex compositions that implement scientific discovery processes.

According to the definition of the Workflow Management Coalition (WFMC, 1999; Hollingsworth, 1995), a workflow is "the automation of a business process, in whole or part, during which documents, information or tasks are passed from one participant to another for action, according to a set of procedural rules." The same definition can be used for scientific processes composed of several processing steps that are connected together to express data and/or control dependencies (Liu et al., 2004). The term process here indicates a set of tasks linked together with the goal of creating a product, calculating a result, or providing a service. Hence, each task (or activity) represents a piece of work that forms one logical step of the overall process (Georgako-poulos et al., 1995).

A workflow is a well defined, possibly a repeatable pattern, or systematic organization of activities designed to achieve a certain transformation of data. Workflows, as practiced in scientific computing, derive from several significant precedent programming models that are worth noting because they have greatly influenced the way we think about workflows in scientific applications. We can call them the dataflow models, in which data is streamed from one actor to another. Although the pure dataflow concept is extremely elegant, it is very hard to make it work in practice because distributing control in a parallel or distributed system can create applications that are not very fault tolerant.

Consequently, many workflow systems use a dataflow model for expressing computation as it can have an implicit centralized control program that sequences and schedules each step. An important benefit of workflows is that, once defined, they can be stored and retrieved for modifications and/or re-execution. This allows users to define typical patterns and reuse them in different scenarios (Bowers et al., 2006). The definition, creation, and execution of workflows are supported by a WMS. A key function of the WMS during a workflow's execution (or enactment) is coordinating the operations of the individual activities, which constitute the workflow.

Through the integrated use of computer science methods and scientific discovery processes, science progressed into a new era where scientific methods changed significantly by the use of computational methods, and new data analysis strategies created the e-science paradigm (Bell et al., 2009). For example, the Pan-STARRS astronomical survey (Deelman et al., 2009) uses workflows from Microsoft Trident Scientific Workflow Workbench to load and validate telescope detections running at about 30 TB/year. Similarly, the USC Epigenome Center is currently using the Pegasus workflow system to exploit the Illumina Genetic Analyzer (GA) system to generate high throughput DNA sequence data (up to eight billion nucleotides per week) to map the epigenetic state of human cells on a genome-wide scale. In this scenario, scientific work-flows demonstrate their effectiveness for programming at high-level complex scientific applications that in general run on supercomputers or on distributed computing infrastructures such as grids, peer-to-peer systems and clouds (Sonntag et al., 2010; Yu and Buyya, 2005; Al-Sha-karchi et al., 2007).

### 3.2.1 Workflow Programming
A main issue in WMSs is the programming structure provided to the developers who implement a scientific application. While some systems provide a textual programming interface, others are based on a visual programming interface. These two different interfaces imply different programming approaches.

Often a scientific workflow is programmed as a graph of several data and processing nodes that include predefined procedures writ-ten in programming languages such as Java, C++, Perl, Python, etc. According to this approach, a scientific workflow is a methodology to orchestrate predefined programs that run single tasks, but are composed together to represent a complex application that gener-ally needs large resources to run and may take a long running time to complete. For an introduction, refer to the work by Taylor et al. (2007), which provides a taxonomy of the main features of scientific workflows. In fact, it is not rare to have scientific workflows, for example in the astronomy domain or in bioinformatics (Cannataro et al., 2004), which take several days or weeks to complete their ex-ecution.

Workflow tasks can be composed together following a number of different patterns, whose variety helps designers addressing the needs of a wide range of application scenarios. A comprehensive collection of workflow patterns, focusing on the description of control flow depen-dencies among tasks, has been described in (van der Aalst et al., 2003). The most common programming structure used in WMSs is the directed acyclic graph (DAG) (Figure 3.3) or its extension that includes loops, which is the directed cyclic graph (DCG).

Of the many possible ways to distinguish workflow computations, one is to consider a simple complexity scale. At the most basic level one

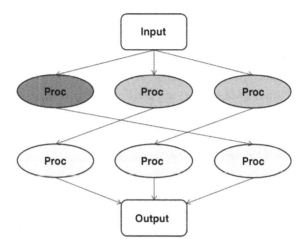

*Fig. 3.3. A simple DAG including data and control nodes.*

can consider linear workflows, in which a sequence of tasks must be performed in a specified linear order. The first task transforms an initial data object into new data object, which is used as input in the next data-transformation task. The execution of the entire chain of tasks may take a few minutes, or it may take days, depending on the computational grain of each single task in the pipeline. When the execution time is short, the most common workflow-programming tool is a simple script written, for instance, in Python, Perl, or Matlab. The case of longer running workflows often requires more sophisticated tools or programming languages.

At the next level of complexity, one can consider workflows that can be represented by a DAG, where nodes of the graph represent tasks to be performed and edges represent dependencies between tasks. Two main types of dependencies can be considered: data dependencies (where the output of a task is used as input by the next tasks) and control dependencies (where before to start one or a set of tasks some tasks must be completed). This is harder to represent with a scripting language without a substantial additional framework behind it, but it is not at all difficult to represent with a tool like Ant. It is the foundation of the Directed Acyclic Graph Manager (DAGMan), a meta-scheduler of Condor (Litzkow et al., 1988), which is a specialized workload management system developed by the University of Wisconsin, and the execution engine of Pegasus. Applications that follow this pattern can be characterized by workflows, in which some tasks depend upon the completion of several other tasks that may be executed concurrently (Deelman et al., 2009).

A DAG can be used to represent a set of programs where the input, output, or execution of one or more programs is dependent on one or more other programs. According to this model, also in DAGMan programs are nodes in the graph, the edges (arcs) identify the program dependencies. For task execution, Condor finds computers for the execution of programs, but it does not schedule programs based on dependencies (Couvares et al., 2007). DAGMan submits tasks to Condor in an order represented by a DAG and processes the task results. An input file defined prior to submission describes the workflow as a DAG, and Condor uses a description file for each program in the DAG. DAGMan is responsible for scheduling, recovery, and reporting for the set of programs submitted to Condor.

The next level of workflow complexity can be characterized by cyclic graphs, where cycles represent some form of implicit or explicit loop or iteration control mechanisms. In this case, the workflow graph often describes a network of tasks where the nodes are either services, some form of software component instances, or represent more abstract control objects. The graph edges represent messages, data streams, or pipes that exchange work or information among services and components.

The highest level of workflow structure is one in which a compact graph model is inappropriate. This is the case when the graph is simply too large and complex to be effectively designed. However, some tools allow one to turn a graph into a new first-class component or service, which can then be included as a node in another graph (a workflow of workflows or hierarchical workflow). This technique allows graphs of arbitrary complexity to be constructed. This nested-workflow approach requires the use of more sophisticated tools both at the composition stage and at the execution stage. In particular, this approach makes the task-to-resource mapping and the task scheduling harder during the workflow execution done on a large scale distributed or parallel infrastructures such as HPC systems or cloud computing platforms (Mirto et al., 2010).

In the case of workflow enactment, two issues must be taken into account: efficiency and robustness. In terms of efficiency, the critical issue is the ability to quickly bind workflow tasks to the appropriate computing resources. It heavily depends on the mechanisms used to assign data to tasks, to move data between tasks that need them at various stages of the enactment. For instance, considering a service-oriented scenario, we cannot assume that Web service protocols like SOAP should be used in anything other than task/service control and simple message delivery (Zhang et al., 2007; Lin et al., 2008). Complex and/or data movement between components of the workflow must be either via an interaction with a data movement service, or through specialized binary-level data channel running directly between the tasks involved.

Robustness is another issue, making the reasonable assumption that some parts of a workflow may fail. It is essential that exception handling must include mechanisms to recover from failure as well as to detect it. Besides, failure is something that can happen to a workflow enactment engine. A related issue is the monitoring of the workflow. Additionally, while restarting a workflow from a failure checkpoint, a user may wish to track the progress of enactment. In some cases the workflow is event driven, and a log of these events that trigger the workflow processing can be analyzed to understand how the workflow is progressing. This is also an important aspect of debugging a workflow. A user may wish to execute the workflow step-by-step to understand the potential errors in the flow logic.

Tools and programming interfaces for scientific workflow composition are important components of workflow systems. Through tools and interfaces, a developer can compose her/his scientific workflow and express details about data sources, task dependencies, resource availability, and other design or execution constraints. Most scientific workflow systems offer graphical interfaces that offer high-level mechanisms for composition, although a few systems exhibit traditional text-based programming interfaces. Workflow users exploit the features of the interfaces that scientific workflow systems expose in order to build their workflows. This corresponds to the design stage of a workflow. In general terms, two main workflow levels can be found in this regard, though there are other approaches that even differentiate more abstraction levels:

- *Abstract workflows*: at this high level of abstraction a workflow contains just information about what have to be done at each task along with information about how tasks are interconnected. There is no notion of how input data is actually delivered or how tasks are implemented.

- *Concrete workflows*: the mapping stage to a concrete workflow annotates each of the tasks with information about the implementation and/or resources to be used. Information about method invocation and actual data exchange format are also defined.

In case a user is familiar with the technology and resources available, they can even specify concrete workflows directly. Once a workflow specification is produced, it is sent to the workflow engine for the execution phase. At this stage, workflow tasks are mapped also onto third-party, distributed, and heterogeneous resources and the scientific computations are accomplished (Juve and Deelman, 2008).

## 3.2.2 Workflow Management Systems

As discussed earlier in this section, WMSs are software environments providing tools to define, compose, map, and execute workflows. There are several WMSs on the market, most of them targeted to a specific application domain. Here we focus on some significant WMSs developed by the research community, with the goal of identifying the most important features and solutions that have been proposed for workflow management in the domain of data analysis.

Although a standard workflow language like Business Process Execution Language (Juric, 2006) has been defined, scientific workflow systems often have developed their own workflow model for allowing users to represent workflows. Other than BPEL, other formalisms like UML, Petri nets (Guan et al., 2006), and XML-based languages (Atay et al., 2007) are used to express workflows. This feature makes it difficult to share workflow specifications and limits interoperability among workflow-based applications that are developed by using different WMSs. Nevertheless, there are some historical reasons for that, as many scientific workflow systems and their workflow models were developed before BPEL existed (Andrews et al., 2003).

WMSs are very useful in solving complex problems and offering real solutions for improving the way business analysis and scientific discovery is done in all domains, as discussed further. Solutions adopted are useful for taking into account new WMSs and represent features that workflow systems must include to support users in scientific application development.

Existing workflow models can be grouped roughly into two main classes:

- *Script-like systems*: where workflow descriptions specify workflows by means of a textual programming language that can be described by a grammar in an analogous way to traditional programming languages such as Perl, Ruby, or Java. They often have complex semantics and an extensive syntax. These types of descriptions declare tasks and parameters by means of a textual specification. Typically, data dependencies can be established between them by annotations. These languages contain specific workflow constructs, such as sequences, loops, while–do, or parallel constructs in order to build up a workflow. Examples of script workflow descriptions are JS4Cloud, Swift, and Karajan. A commonly used script-based approach to describe workflows, mainly in the business workflow community, is BPEL and its version for Web services that builds on IBM's Web Service Flow Language, WSFL.
- *Graphical-based systems*: where workflow models specify the workflow with only a few basic graphical elements that correspond to the graph components such as nodes and edges. Compared with script-based descriptions, graphical-based systems are easier to use and more intuitive for the unskilled user mainly because of graphical representation. While the nodes typically represent workflow tasks, communications (or data dependencies) between different tasks are represented as links going from one node to another. Workflow systems that support graph-based models often incorporate graphical user interfaces (GUIs) that allow users to model workflows by dragging and dropping graph elements. Purely graph-based workflow descriptions generally utilize DAGs. As mentioned, DAG-based languages offer a limited expressiveness, so that they cannot represent complex workflows (e.g., loops cannot be expressed directly).

### 3.2.3 Workflow Management Systems for Clouds

Several systems have been designed to develop scientific and data analysis workflows on high performance computing systems using script-based or visual formalisms (Talia, 2013). Some of them have been implemented on parallel computing systems, other on grids, recently some have made available on clouds (Hidders et al., 2015). In the following, we shortly discuss the most representative WMSs that support either script-based or visual workflow design and implementation in cloud environments such as Pegasus, Taverna, Kepler, WS-PGRADE, CloudFlows, E-Science Central, Data Mining Cloud Framework (DMCF), COMPSs, and Swift. Some of these systems (Pegasus, Swift, ClowdFlows) and – in more detail – DMCF, will be further discussed in Chapter 4.

Pegasus (Deelman et al., 2009), developed at the University of Southern California, includes a set of technologies to execute workflow-based applications in a number of different environments, including desktops, clusters, and grids. It has been used in several scientific areas including bioinformatics, astronomy, earthquake science, gravitational wave physics, and ocean science. The Pegasus WMS can manage the execution of an application formalized as a visual workflow by mapping it onto available resources and executing the workflow tasks in the order of their dependencies.

Taverna (Wolstencroft, 2013) is a WMS developed at the University of Manchester. Its primary goal is supporting the life sciences community (biology, chemistry, and medicine) to design and execute scientific workflows and support *in silico* experimentation, where research is performed through computer simulations with models closely reflecting the real world. Even though most Taverna applications lie in the bioinformatics domain, it can be applied to a wide range of fields since it can invoke any REST or SOAP-based Web service. This feature is very useful to allow users of Taverna to reuse code (represented as a service) that is available on the Internet. Taverna can orchestrate Web services and these may be running in the cloud, but this is transparent for Taverna, as demonstrated in the BioVel project.

Kepler (Ludäscher et al., 2006) is a graphical WMS that has been used in several projects to manage, process, and analyze scientific data.

Kepler provides a GUI for designing scientific workflows, which are a structured set of tasks linked together that implement a computational solution to a scientific problem. Data is encapsulated in messages or tokens, and transferred between tasks through input and output ports. Kepler provides an assortment of built-in components with a major focus on statistical analysis and supports task parallel execution of workflows using multiple threads on a single machine.

WS-PGRADE (Kacsuk et al., 2012) is a general-purpose WMS that allows users to create and run workflows on distributed computing systems such as grid and cloud platforms. The system allows users to define workflows through a graphical interface and to execute them on different distributed computing infrastructures (DCIs), including popular cloud systems such as Amazon EC2 and Google App Engine. The visual formalism expresses parallelism through parallel paths or through parametric input nodes. A parametric input node will be executed in as many instances as many files arrive on its port. End-users may use the system through a simplified interface where they can download a workflow from a repository, configure its parameter, and launch and monitor its execution on the underlying DCI.

ClowdFlows (Kranjc et al., 2012) is a cloud-based platform for the composition, execution, and sharing of interactive data mining workflows. According with the Software as a Service approach, ClowdFlows provides a user interface that allows programming visual workflows in any Web browser. Additionally, its service-oriented architecture allows third party services (e.g., Web services wrapping open-source or custom data mining algorithms). The server side consists of methods for the client side workflow editor to compose and execute workflows, and a relational database of workflows and data.

E-Science Central (e-SC) (Hiden et al., 2013) is a system that allows scientists to store, analyze, and share data in the Cloud. Like ClowdFlows, e-SC provides a user interface that allows programming visual workflows in any Web browser. Its in-browser workflow editor allows users to design a workflow by connecting services, either uploaded by themselves or shared by other users of the system. One of the most common use cases for e-SC is to provide a data-analysis back end to a standalone desktop or Web application. To this end, the e-SC API provides a set of workflow control methods and data structures. In the current implementation, all the workflow services within a single invocation of a workflow execute on the same cloud node.

Differently from the systems above, which support visual workflow design, the Data Mining Cloud Framework (DMCF) provides both visual and script-based workflow programming with the JS-4Cloud script language and the VL4Cloud visual formalism, so as to meet the needs of both high level users and who prefer to program. Moreover, DMCF natively supports the execution of workflow tasks on distributed environments composed by multiple machines, and is able to parallelize the execution of the tasks of each workflow, an important feature to ensure scalable data analysis workflows execution on the cloud.

COMPSs (Marozzo et al., 2012a) is a programming model and an execution runtime, whose main objective is to ease the development of workflows for distributed environments, including private and public clouds. With COMPSs, users create a sequential application and specify which methods of the application code will be executed remotely. Providing an annotated interface where these methods are declared with some metadata about them and their parameters does this selection. The runtime intercepts any call to a selected method creating a representative task and finding the data dependencies with all the previous ones during application execution.

Swift (Wilde et al., 2011) is a parallel scripting language that runs workflows across several distributed systems, like clusters, clouds, grids, and supercomputers. It provides a functional language in which workflows are modeled as a set of program invocations with their associated command-line arguments, input and output files. Swift uses a C-like syntax consisting of function definitions and expressions that provide an implicit data-driven task parallelism. The runtime comprises a set of services that implement the parallel execution of Swift scripts exploiting the maximal concurrency permitted by data dependencies within a script and by external resource availability.

## 3.3 NoSQL MODELS FOR DATA ANALYTICS

With the exponential growth of data to be stored in distributed network scenarios, relational databases exhibit scalability limitations that significantly reduce the efficiency of querying and analysis (Abramova et al., 2014). In fact, most relational databases have little ability to scale horizontally over many servers, which makes challenging storing and managing the huge amounts of data produced everyday by many applications.

The *NoSQL* or *non-relational* database approach became popular in the last years as an alternative or as a complement to relational databases, in order to ensure horizontal scalability of simple read/write database operations distributed over many servers (Cattell, 2010). Compared to relational databases, NoSQL databases are generally more flexible and scalable, as they are capable of taking advantage of new nodes transparently, without requiring manual distribution of information or additional database management (Stonebraker, 2010). Since database management may be a challenging task with huge amounts of data, NoSQL databases are designed to ensure automatic data distribution and fault tolerance (Gajendran, 2012).

In the remainder of this section, we introduce the key features of the NoSQL approach, provide a classification of NoSQL databases, describe some representative NoSQL systems, and discuss some use cases for NoSQL databases, with a focus on data analytics.

### 3.3.1 Key Features of NoSQL

According to Cattell (2010), Not Only SQL (NoSQL) systems are generally characterized by six key features:

- The capability to horizontally scale simple operations over many servers
- The support to replication and partitioning of data over many servers
- A simple call level interface, in contrast to an SQL binding
- An efficient use of distributed indexes and RAM for data storage
- The capability to dynamically add new attributes to data records
- Do not provide ACID transactional properties of most relational databases

The first feature emphasizes the need to provide *horizontal scalability* on *simple operations*, for example, reading or writing a small number of records in each operation. This happens, for instance, in applications searching and updating multiserver databases of personal profiles, Web postings, and customer records. The term horizontal scalability refers to the capability of distributing both data and load of these simple operations over many servers, with no RAM or disks shared among the servers.

Support to replication and partitioning is a key feature to ensure both fault tolerance and scalability. Most NoSQL systems allow *sharding*, that is the horizontal partitioning of data by storing records on different servers according to some key. Some systems also allow vertical partitioning, which stores parts of a single record on different servers.

Regarding the third key feature, even if most NoSQL databases provide a simple call level interface, in contrast to Structured Query Language (SQL), which is the language most commonly associated with relational databases, partial support to SQL-based querying is possible even though the underlying database is not relational.

The fourth key feature usually associated with NoSQL databases is an efficient use of distributed indexes and volatile memory for data processing. In particular, since I/O data access is relatively slow, mapping data into RAM increases performance and reduces the time necessary for querying. In addition, in-memory processing can be highly scalable, because data can be replicated and partitioned over the RAM of multiple servers.

In contrast to relational databases, NoSQL databases are schemaless, which means that new data items can be stored even if they do not adhere to a predefined structure. This is another key feature of NoSQL databases, as it provides applications with the ability to dynamically add new attributes to data records, without modifications to predefined schemas.

Finally, NoSQL databases generally do not satisfy the atomicity, consistency, isolation, and durability (ACID) properties of most relational databases. On the other hand, most NoSQL databases adhere to the basically available, soft state, and eventually consistent (BASE) principle, which is characterized by high availability of data, while sacrificing its consistency (Abramova et al., 2014; Pritchett, 2008; Cook, 2009). The BASE principle derives from the CAP theorem (Gilbert and Lynch, 2002), which states that a distributed system can have only two out of three of the following properties: consistency (C), availability (A), and partition tolerance (P). The NoSQL systems generally give up strong consistency, which is hard to achieve across multiple servers, in favor of availability and partition tolerance. According to the BASE principle, most NoSQL databases provide *eventual consistency*, meaning that updates are *eventually* propagated to all nodes.

### 3.3.2 Classification of NoSQL Databases

NoSQL databases provide ways to store scalar values (e.g., numbers, strings), binary objects (e.g., images, videos), or more complex values. According to their data model, NoSQL databases can be grouped into three main categories (Cattell, 2010): *key-value stores, document stores, extensible record stores*.

- *Key-value stores*: provide mechanisms to store data as (*key, value*) pairs over multiple servers. In these databases, a distributed hash table (DHT) can be used to implement a scalable indexing structure, where data retrieval is performed by using *key* to find *value*. However, key-value stores typically go beyond the standard insert, delete, and lookup operations primitives of DHTs, by providing additional functionalities for replication, versioning, locking, transactions, sorting, and other features (Cattell, 2010).
- *Document stores*: are designed to manage data stored in documents that use different formats (e.g., JSON), where each document is assigned a unique key that is used to identify and retrieve the document. Therefore, document stores extend key-value stores because they provide for storing, retrieving, and managing semistructured information, rather than single values. Unlike the key-value stores, document stores generally support secondary indexes and multiple types of documents per database, and provide mechanisms to query collections based on multiple attribute value constraints (Cattell, 2010).
- *Extensible record stores*: also called *Wide column stores,* provide mechanisms to store *extensible records* that can be partitioned

across multiple servers. In this type of database, records are said to be *extensible* because new attributes can be added on a per record basis. Extensible record stores provide both horizontal partitioning (storing records on different nodes) and vertical partitioning (storing parts of a single record on different servers). In some systems, columns of a table can be distributed over multiple servers by using *column groups*, where predefined groups indicate the columns that are best stored together.

### 3.3.3 NoSQL Systems

There are currently tens of NoSQL databases in the market, each one with different solutions and optimizations. In the following we present three examples of NoSQL databases belonging to the three main categories introduced earlier: Amazon's Dynamo (De Candia et al., 2007) as an example of key-value store; MongoDB (Plugge et al., 2010) as an example of document store; and Google's Bigtable (Chang et al., 2006) as an example of extensible record store. These databases will be shortly described based on their data model, query model, architecture, replication and partitioning strategies, consistency model, and failure handling.

#### 3.3.3.1 Dynamo

Developed by Amazon to support its services, Dynamo is one of the most important NoSQL systems that has influenced the design of several other key-value stores.

- *Data model*: Dynamo adopts a simple *key-value* data model, in which values are stored as binary objects. Despite its simplicity, this is a very effective data model for services like product catalogue management, where operations are mostly limited to objects that can be accessed by key.
- *Query model*: Dynamo provides a simple querying interface that reflects the underlying data model. Basically, two operations are available: *get*, to retrieve an object given its key, and *put,* to store an object with associated key.
- *Architecture*: Dynamo adopts a "shared nothing" architecture, without any master or shared file system. Servers are linked to each other to form a ring overlay, in which every server has the ability to route requests for any key to the appropriate server. The ring topology and associated routing strategy ensures load balancing and scalability.

- *Replication and partitioning*: given an object and its key, the object is first stored on the server responsible for the interval in which the key lies. Then, the server forwards a replication message to a predefined number of its successors along the ring. In this way, the object is replicated on a number of nodes, all of which has the ability of returning that object given the corresponding key. Data partitioning is based on a variant of the consistent hashing technique typically adopted in DHTs.
- *Consistency*: the Dynamo database is eventually consistent. All the write operations are completed immediately without waiting that all replicas have received the update. Thus, no commit is required on concurrent writes. Sequential reads may return different values if made on different replicas. For this reason, Dynamo implements Multi-Version Concurrency Control (MVCC), which creates a new immutable version of an object after each write. In fact, when an MVCC database updates a data element, it does not overwrite the old value of that data element with new data, but instead it marks the old data as obsolete and adds the newer *version*.
- *Failure handling*: Dynamo implements a *gossip*-based strategy that allows every node to notify all the other nodes in the ring about topological variations, and the consequent necessity of keys-to-nodes remapping, originated by nodes leaving the network for a failure.

### 3.3.3.2 MongoDB

MongoDB is one of the most popular NoSQL databases based on documents, which can also be used to store and distribute large binary files such as images or video.

- *Data model*: in MongoDB, documents are saved in Binary JSON (BSON) format, which is an extension of JSON with support for additional types. The internal structure of documents is not tied to a scheme. Therefore, applications can add or remove a field without limitations. Besides documents, MongoDB introduces the concept of Collection that allows grouping similar documents together.
- *Query model*: client applications can communicate with MongoDB through a driver that handles interactions with an appropriate language. Similarly, as in the case for relational databases, the driver

supports Create, Read, Update, and Delete (CRUD) operations, which are specified through a document in BSON format.

- *Architecture*: the architecture of MongoDB includes three main components: shards, routers, and config servers. Shards are the nodes that store the data in the form of chunks. Routers interface with client applications and route operations to the appropriate shards. Config server keep track of which chunks is responsible each shard in the network.

- *Replication and partitioning*: to ensure reliability and availability, shards are typically organized in clusters with internal replication. Within a sharded cluster, partitioning is enabled on a per-database basis. After enabling sharding for a database, it is possible to choose which collections to shard. For each sharded collection, a shard key determines the distribution of the collection's documents among the cluster's shards.

- *Consistency*: MongoDB does not support multidocument transactions. However, it provides atomic operations on a single document. In many cases, these document-level atomic operations are sufficient to solve problems that would require ACID transactions in a relational database.

- *Failure handling*: MongoDB has different behaviors depending on the type of failure that has occurred in the system. For example, the failure of a replica does not affect availability because write operations are always assigned to the primary node of a cluster. If it is the primary node to fail, however, data remains temporarily unreachable until a new primary is elected.

### 3.3.3.3 Bigtable

Designed by Google, Bigtable is one of the most popular extensible record stores. Built above the Google File System, it is used in many services with different needs: some require low latencies to ensure the real-time response to users, and other more oriented to the analysis of large volumes of data.

- *Data model*: data in Bigtable are stored in sparse, distributed, persistent, multidimensional tables. Each value is an uninterpreted array of bytes indexed by a triplet (row key, column key, and timestamp). Data are maintained in lexicographic order by row key. The row range for a table is dynamically partitioned. Each row range is called a *tablet*, which is the unit of distribution and load balancing. Column keys are grouped into sets called *column families*. All data stored in the same column family are usually of the same type.

- *Query model*: Bigtable provides a C++ library that allows users to filter data based on row keys, column keys, and timestamps. It provides functions for creating and deleting tables and column families. The library allows clients to write or delete values in a table, look up values from individual rows, or iterate over subsets of data in a table.

- *Architecture*: Bigtable includes several components. The *Google File System* (*GFS*) is used to store log and data files. *Chubby* provides a highly-available and persistent distributed lock service. Each tablet is assigned to one *Tablet server*, and each tablet server typically manages up to a thousand tablets. A *Master server* is responsible for assigning tablets to tablet servers, detecting the addition or expiration of tablet servers, and balancing the load among tablet servers.

- *Replication and partitioning*: partitioning is based on the tablet concept introduced earlier. A tablet can have a maximum of one server that runs it and there may be periods of time in which it is not assigned to any server, and therefore cannot be reached by the client application. Bigtable does not directly manage replication because it requires that each tablet is assigned to a single server, but uses the GFS distributed file system that provides replication of tablets as files called SSTables.

- *Consistency*: the partitioning strategy assigns each tablet to one server. This allows Bigtable to provide strong consistency at the expense of availability in the presence of failures on a server. Operations on a single row are atomic, and can support even transactions on blocks of operations. Transactions across multiple rows must be managed on the client side.

- *Failure handling*: when a tablet server starts, it creates a file with a unique name in a default directory in the Chubby space and acquires exclusive lock. The master periodically checks whether the servers still have the lock on their files. If not, the master assumes the servers have failed and marks the associated tablets as unassigned, making them ready for reassignment to other servers.

## 3.3.4 Use Cases

The various features of NoSQL databases discussed here are particularly useful to perform data analysis on large data volumes.

Key-value stores can be one of the most effective solutions to perform real time analysis in scenarios where operations are mostly limited to objects, which can be accessed by key, due to the fact that these databases are very fast in retrieving items given their key. The case of Amazon's Dynamo shows that key-value store are particularly appropriate for e-commerce systems where is necessary to store and manage huge amount of data about products, customer preferences, shopping carts, sales rank and session management. This enables a wide range of analytics to be performed on such data, such as association rule learning aimed at uncovering connections between objects such as customers, sellers and products.

Document stores such as MongoDB are an effective choice to store and process documents of any structure, such as events data, time series data, text, and binary data. Through sharding, huge amounts of data can be horizontally partitioned across a large number of commodity servers, with complete application transparency, that is, without requiring users to build custom partitioning and caching layers. This scalability enables powerful analytics to be performed in real time, by exploiting distribution of data and computation. For example, MongoDB can run complex *ad hoc* analytics, thanks to its query support, which includes secondary, geospatial, and text search indexes, as well as native support to MapReduce.

Use cases for extensible record stores are similar to those for document stores, with multiple types of objects that can be queried by any field. However, extensible record store systems are generally aimed at higher throughput, and may provide stronger concurrency guarantees, at the cost of slightly more complexity than document stores (Cattell, 2010). A well-known example of data analytics service built on top of an extensible record store is Google Analytics, which uses Bigtable (Chang et al., 2006). Google Analytics provides aggregate statistics about web sites, such as the number of unique visitors per day, page views per day, as well as site-tracking reports, such as the percentage of customers who made a purchase, given the total number of page visitors. Whenever a page is visited, Google Analytics records a user identified and information about the page being fetched. Google Analytics summarizes this data and makes it available to webmasters. The service makes use of two tables. The raw click table maintains a row for each end-user session. The summary table contains various summaries for each website, generated from the raw click table by MapReduce jobs executed on a periodic basis.

## 3.4 SUMMARY

The development of data analysis applications on cloud computing systems is a complex task that needs to exploit smart software solutions and innovative technologies. Such software tools, frameworks, and solutions allow clouds to play as enablers for big data analytics by implementing the data-analysis-as-a-service model. The software tools and technologies we presented in this chapter are based on three paradigms and associated tools, which represent the main pillars for developing scalable data analysis on clouds: MapReduce, workflow systems, and NoSQL database management systems.

MapReduce is widely used to implement scalable data analysis algorithms and applications executed on multiple machines, to efficiently analyze big amounts of data. Hadoop is the best-known MapReduce implementation and it is commonly used to develop scalable applications analyzing big amounts of data. As discussed, Hadoop is also a reference tool for several other frameworks, such as Storm, Hive, Oozie, and Spark. Moreover, besides Hadoop and its ecosystem, several other MapReduce implementations have been implemented within other systems, including GridGain, Skynet, MapSharp, and Disco. Despite the scalability and large availability of MapReduce solutions, in some cases more general tools are needed to develop irregular concurrent data analysis applications that cannot be expressed as a combination of *map* and *reduce* functions. In those cases, systems based on the workflow paradigm are often used. For this reason, in the past years, many efforts have been done to develop distributed WMSs for complex data-driven applications. Workflows provide a declarative way of specifying the high level logic of an application, hiding the low level details. They are also able to integrate existing software modules, datasets, and services in complex compositions that implement discovery processes. Here we discussed the workflow programming models and presented several WMSs, which have been implemented on clouds and are used to develop scalable data analysis applications. Finally, we also discussed NoSQL database technology that became popular in the last few years, as an alternative or complement to relational databases. In fact, NoSQL systems in several application scenarios are more scalable and provide higher performance than relational databases. We introduced the basic principles of NoSQL, described representative NoSQL systems, and outlined interesting data analytics use cases where NoSQL tools are useful.

## REFERENCES

Abramova, V., Bernardino, J., Furtado, P., 2014. Which NoSQL database? A performance overview. OJDB 1 (2).

Al-Shakarchi, E., Cozza, P., Harrison, A., Mastroianni, C., Shields, M., Talia, D., Taylor, I., 2007. Distributing workflows over a ubiquitous P2P network. Sci. Prog. 15 (4), 269–281.

Andrews, T., Curbera, F., Dholakia, H., Goland, Y., Klein, J., Leymann, F., Liu, K., Roller, D., Smith, D., Thatte, S., Trickovic, I., Weerawarana, S., 2003. "Business process execution language for web services". OASIS specification.

Atay, M., Chebotko, A., Liu, D., Lu, S., Fotouhi, F., 2007. Efficient schema-based XML-to-relational data mapping. Inform. Syst. 32 (3), 458–476.

Bell, G., Hey, T., Szalay, A., 2009. Beyond the data deluge. Science 323 (5919), 1297–1298.

Bowers, S., Ludaescher, B., Ngu, A., Critchlow, T., 2006. Enabling scientific workflow reuse through structured composition of dataflow and control-flow. In: Proceedings of the Twenty-Second International Conference on Data Engineering Workshops (ICDEW'06). Washington, DC.

Cannataro, M., Guzzo, A., Comito, C., Veltri, P., 2004. Ontology-based design of bioinformatics workflows on PROTEUS. JDIM 2 (1), 87–92, Digital Information Research Foundation (DIRF) Press.

Cary, A., Sun, Z., Hristidis, V., Rishe, N., 2009. Experiences on processing spatial data with MapReduce. In: Winslett, M. (Ed.), In: Proceedings of the twenty-first International Conference on Scientific, Statistical Database Management (SSDBM'09), Springer- Verlag, Berlin, Heidelberg, pp. 302–319.

Cattell, R., 2010. Scalable SQL and NoSQL data stores. SIGMOD Record 39 (4), 12–27.

Chang, F., Dean, J., Ghemawat, S., Hsieh, W.C., Wallach, D.A., Burrows, M., Chandra, T., Fikes, A., Gruber, R., 2006. Bigtable: a distributed storage system for structured data. OSDI 2006.

Chu, C., Kim, S.K., Lin, Y.A., Yu, Y., Bradski, G., Ng, A.Y., Olukotun, K., 2007. Map-reduce for machine learning on multicore. Advances in neural information processing systems 19, 281.

Coleman, R., Ghattamaneni, U., Logan, M., Labouseur, A., 2012. Computational finance with Map-Reduce in Scala. Conference on Parallel and Distributed Processing (PDPTA'12). Las Vegas, NV, pp. 16–19.

Cook, J.D., 2009. ACID versus BASE for database transactions. http://www.johndcook.com/blog/2009/07/06/brewer-cap-theorem-base/.

Couvares, P., Kosar, T., Roy, A., Weber, J., Wenger, K., 2007. Workflow management in Condor. Workflows for e-Science. Springer, New York, pp. 357–375.

Das, S., Sismanis, Y., Beyer, K.S., Gemulla, R., Haas, P.J., McPherson, J., 2010. Ricardo: Integrating R and Hadoop. In: Proceedings of the 2010 ACM SIGMOD International Conference on Management of Data (SIGMOD '10) ACM. New York, NY, USA, pp. 987–998.

De Candia, G., Hastorun, D., Jampani, M., Kakulapati, G., Lakshman, A., Pilchin, A., Sivasubramanian, S., Vosshall, P., Vogels, W., 2007. Dynamo: Amazon's highly available key-value store. In: Proceedings of Twenty-First ACM SIGOPS Symposium on Operating Systems Principles (SOSP '07), ACM. New York, NY, USA, pp. 205–220.

Dean, J., Ghemawat, S., 2004. MapReduce: Simplified data processing on large clusters. Sixth USENIX Symposium on Operating Systems Design and Implementation (OSDI'04). San Francisco, USA.

Dean, J., Ghemawat, S., 2008. MapReduce: simplified data processing on large clusters. Communications of the ACM 51 (1), 107–113.

Dou, A., Kalogeraki, V., Gunopulos, D., Mielikainen, T., Tuulos, V.H., 2010. Misco: A MapReduce Framework for Mobile Systems. Third International Conference on Pervasive Technologies Related to Assistive Environments (PETRA'10). New York, USA.

Deelman, E., Gannon, D., Shields, M., Taylor, I., 2009. Workflows and e-Science: an overview of workflow system features and capabilities. Future Gener. Comp. Syst. 25 (5), 528–540.

Ekanayake, J., Pallickara, S., Fox, G., 2008. Mapreduce for data intensive scientific analyses. Fourth IEEE International Conference on e-Science (e-Science'08). Indianapolis, USA, pp. 277–284.

Ekanayake, J., Li, H., Zhang, B., Gunarathne, T., Bae, S.-H., Qiu, J., Fox, G., 2010. Twister: a runtime for iterative MapReduce. First International Workshop on MapReduce and its Applications (MAPREDUCE'10). Chicago, USA, pp. 110–119.

Fedak, G., He, H., Cappello, F., 2009. BitDew: A data management and distribution service with multi-protocol and reliable file transfer. J. Netw. Comput. Appl. 32 (5), 961–975.

Gajendran, S., 2012. A Survey on NoSQL Databases, http://ping.sg/story/A-Survey-on-NoSQL-Databases–Department-of-Computer-Science.

Georgakopoulos, D., Hornick, M., Sheth, A., 1995. An overview of workflow management: from process modeling to workflow automation infrastructure. Distrib. Parallel Dat. 3 (2), 119–153.

Gilbert, S., Lynch, N., 2002. Brewer's conjecture and the feasibility of consistent, available, and partition-tolerant web services. ACM SIGACT News 33 (2), 51–59.

Gongqing, W., Haiguang, L., Xuegang, H., Yuanjun, B., Jing, Z., Xindong, W., 2009. MReC4.5: C4.5 ensemble classification with MapReduce. ChinaGrid Annual Conference, 2009. ChinaGrid '09. China, vol. 4, pp. 249, 255.

Guan, Z., et al., 2006. Grid-flow: a grid-enabled scientific workflow system with a petri net-based interface. Ph.D. Thesis, University of Alabama at Birmingham.

Guo, Z., Fox, G., Zhou, M., 2012. Investigation of data locality in MapReduce. In: Proceedings of the 2012 Twelfth IEEE/ACM International Symposium on Cluster, Cloud and Grid Computing (CCGRID'12). Washington, DC, USA.

Hidders, J., Missier, P., Sroka, J. (Eds.), 2015. Recent advances in Scalable Workflow Enactment Engines and Technologies. Future Gener. Comp. Syst. 46, 1–2.

Hiden, H., Woodman, S., Watson, P., Cala, J., 2013. Developing cloud applications using the e-Science central platform, philosophical transactions of the royal society A. Math. Phys. Eng. Sci. 371 (1983), 1–12.

Hollingsworth, D., 1995. Workflow management coalition specification: the workflow reference model, Document Number TC00-1003, v. 1.1.

Juric, M.B., 2006. Business Process Execution Language for Web Services BPEL and BPEL4WS, Second ed. Packt Publishing.

Juve, G., Deelman, E., 2008. Resource provisioning options for large-scale scientific workflows. Third International Workshop on Scientific Workflows and Business Workflow Standards in e-Science. Indianapolis, USA.

Kacsuk, P., Farkas, Z., Kozlovszky, M., Hermann, G., Balasko, A., Karoczkai, K., Marton, I., 2012. Ws-pgrade/guse generic dci gateway framework for a large variety of user communities. J. Grid Comp. 10 (4), 601–630.

Kranjc, J., Podpecan, V., Lavrac, N., 2012. ClowdFlows: a cloud based scientific workflow platform. In: Flach, P., Bie, T., Cristianini, N. (Eds.), Machine Learning and Knowledge Discovery in Databases, Lecture Notes in Computer Science, vol. 7524, Springer, Heidelberg, Germany, pp. 816–819.

Lin, C., Lu, S., Lai, Z., Chebotko, A., Fei, X., Hua, J., Fotouhi, F., 2008. Service-oriented architecture for VIEW: a visual scientific workflow management system. In: Proceedings of IEEE International Conference Services Computing (SCC '08). Washington, DC, USA, pp. 335–342.

Lin, H., Ma, X., Archuleta, J., Feng, W.-C., Gardner, M., Zhang, Z., 2010. MOON: MapReduce on opportunistic environments. In: Nineteenth International Symposium on High Performance Distributed Computing (HPDC'10). Chicago, USA.

Lin, M., Lee, P., Hsueh, S., 2012. Apriori-based frequent itemset mining algorithms on MapReduce. In: Proceedings of the Sixth International Conference on Ubiquitous Information Management and Communication (ICUIMC '12). New York, USA.

Liu, L., Pu, C., Ruiz, D., 2004. A systematic approach to flexible specification, composition, and restructuring of workflow activities. J. Dat. Manag. 15 (1), 1–40.

Litzkow, M., Livny, M., Mutka, M., 1988. Condor – a hunter of idle workstations. In: Proceedings of the Eighth International Conference on Distributed Computing Systems, IEEE Computer Society, New York, pp. 104–111.

Ludäscher, B., Altintas, I., Berkley, C., Higgins, D., Jaeger, E., Jones, M., Lee, E., Tao, J., Zhao, Y., 2006. Scientific workflow management and the Kepler system. Concurr. Comput. 18 (10), 1039–1065.

Ma, Q., Yang, B., Qian, W., Zhou, A., 2009. Query processing of massive trajectory data based on mapreduce. In: Proceedings of the First International Workshop on Cloud Data Management (CloudDB '09). New York, NY, USA, pp. 9–16.

Marozzo, F., Lordan, F., Rafanell, R., Lezzi, D., Talia, D., Badia, R.M., 2012a. Enabling cloud interoperability with Compss. In: Proceedings. of the Eighteenth International European Conference on Parallel and Distributed (Europar 2012), vol. 7484. Lecture Notes in Computer Science. Rhodes Island, Greece, pp. 16–27.

Marozzo, F., Talia, D., Trunfio, P., 2012b. P2P-MapReduce: parallel data processing in dynamic Cloud environments. J. Comput. Syst. Sci. 78 (5), 1382–1402.

Mirto, M., Passante, M., Aloisio, G., 2010. A grid meta scheduler for a distributed interoperable workflow management system. In: Proceedings of the 2010 IEEE Twentieth International Symposium on Computer-Based Medical Systems, CBMS'10, IEEE Computer Society. Washington, DC, USA, pp. 138–143.

Plugge, E., Hawkins, T., Membrey, P., 2010. The Definitive Guide to MongoDB: The NoSQL Database for Cloud and Desktop Computing, First ed. Apress, Berkely, CA, USA.

Pritchett, D., 2008. BASE: an acid alternative. ACM Queue 6 (3), 48–55.

Ranger, C., Raghuraman, R., Penmetsa, A., Bradski, G., Kozyrakis, C., 2007. Evaluating MapReduce for multi-core and multiprocessor systems. Thirteenth International Symposium on High-Performance Computer Architecture (HPCA'07). Phoenix, USA.

Sonntag, M., Karastoyanova, D., Deelman, E., 2010. Bridging the gap between business and scientific workflows. In: Proceedings of the Sixth IEEE International Conference on e-Science, IEEE Computer Society.

Stonebraker, M., 2010. SQL databases vs. NoSQL databases. Commun. ACM 53 (4), 10–11.

Sun, Z., Fox, G., 2012. Study on parallel SVM based on MapReduce. International Conference on Parallel and Distributed Processing Techniques and Applications. Las Vegas, USA, pp. 16–19.

Talia, D., 2013. Workflow systems for science: concepts and tools. ISRN Software Engineering.

Tang, J., Sun, J., Wang, C., Yang, Z., 2009. Social influence analysis in large-scale networks. In: Proceedings of the Fifteenth ACM SIGKDD International Conference on Knowledge Discovery and Data Mining (KDD '09). New York, USA.

Tang, B., Moca, M., Chevalier, S., He, H., Fedak, G., 2010. Towards MapReduce for desktop Grid computing. In: Fifth International Conference on P2P, Parallel, Grid, Cloud and Internet Computing (3PGCIC'10). Fukuoka, Japan.

Taylor, I.J., Deelman, E., Gannon, D.B., Shields, M. (Eds.), 2007. Workflows for e-Science: Scientific Workflows for Grids. Springer, London.

van der Aalst, W.M.P., ter Hofstede, A.H.M., Kiepuszewski, B., Barros, A.P., 2003. Workflow patterns. Distrib. Parallel Dat. 14 (1), 5–51.

White, T., 2009. Hadoop: The Definitive Guide, First ed. O'Reilly Media, Inc.

Wilde, M., Hategan, M., Wozniak, J.M., Clifford, B., Katz, D.S., Foster, I., 2011. Swift: a language for distributed parallel scripting. Parallel Comput. 37 (9), 633–652.

Wolstencroft, K., et al., 2013. The Taverna workflow suite: designing and executing workflows of web services on the desktop, web or in the cloud. Nucleic Acids Res. 41 (W1), W557–W561.

Workflow Management Coalition, Terminology and Glossary, Document Number WFMC-TC-1011, Issue 3.0, 1999.

Xin, R.S., Rosen, J., Zaharia, M., Franklin, M.J., Shenker, S., Stoica, I., 2013. Shark: SQL and rich analytics at scale. In: Proceedings of the 2013 ACM SIGMOD International Conference on Management of Data (SIGMOD '13). New York, USA.

Yu, J., Buyya, R., 2005. A taxonomy of scientific workflow systems for grid computing. SIGMOD Record 34 (3), 44–49.

Zhang, L., Zhang, J., Cai, H., 2007. Services Computing. Springer-Verlag, Berlin, Heidelberg.

# CHAPTER 4

# Designing and Supporting Scalable Data Analytics

This chapter presents innovative systems existing on clouds for designing and implementing scalable data analytics applications. Methods for application development based on some of the discussed systems are reported and explained on real application cases. Section 4.1 introduces a series of software frameworks designed and used for implementing data analysis application on clouds systems. Section 4.2 discusses a workflow-based scalable framework and how it can be used for designing scalable data analytics applications on clouds. Section 4.3 presents a workflow-based paradigm and two associated languages for programming data analysis applications on clouds. Finally, Section 4.4 describes a set of data analysis case studies that have been implemented with the programming languages discussed in the previous sections.

## 4.1 DATA ANALYSIS SYSTEMS FOR CLOUDS

Recently several software tools and frameworks have been developed and used for implementing data analysis applications on clouds systems. Here we introduce a selection of those frameworks that have been compiled taking into account features such as impact on the user community, novelty, and performance. Among them we must include the Data Mining Cloud Framework (DMCF), a programming and runtime system for enabling the scalable execution of complex data analysis workflows on clouds, we recently developed, that is presented in more detail in the next sections of this chapter where the DMCF architecture and its programming interfaces are described. In fact, DMCF provides visual and script programming models that allows users to model complex data analysis workflows without worrying about low-level aspects that can be addressed by the runtime system or the cloud platform.

## 4.1.1 Pegasus

As mentioned in the previous chapter, Pegasus is a workflow management system developed at the University of Southern California for supporting the implementation of scientific applications also in the area of data analysis. Pegasus (Deelman et al., 2009) includes a set of software modules to execute workflow-based applications in a number of different environments, including desktops, clouds, clusters, and grids. It has been used in several scientific areas including bioinformatics, astronomy, earthquake science, gravitational wave physics, and ocean science. The Pegasus workflow management system can manage the execution of an application expressed as a visual workflow by mapping it onto available resources and executing the workflow tasks in the order of their dependencies. In particular, significant activities have been recently performed on Pegasus to support the system implementation on cloud platforms and manage computational workflows in the cloud for developing data-intensive scientific applications (Juve et al., 2010) (Nagavaram et al., 2011). The Pegasus system has been used with IaaS clouds for workflow applications and the most recent versions of Pegasus can be used to map and execute workflows on commercial and academic IaaS clouds such as Amazon EC2, Nimbus, OpenNebula, and Eucalyptus (Deelman et al., 2015).

The Pegasus system includes four main components:

- *The Mapper*: which builds an executable workflow based on an abstract workflow provided by a user or generated by the workflow composition system. To this end, this component finds the appropriate software, data, and computational resources required for workflow execution. The Mapper can also restructure the workflow in order to optimize performance, and add transformations for data management or to generate provenance information.
- *The Execution Engine* (*DAGMan*): which executes in appropriate order the tasks defined in the workflow. This component relies on the compute, storage, and network resources defined in the executable workflow to perform the necessary activities. It includes a local component and some remote ones.
- *The Task Manager*: which is in charge of managing single workflow tasks by supervising their execution on local and/or remote resources.

- *The Monitoring Component*: which monitors the workflow execution, analyzes the workflow and job logs and stores them into a workflow database used to collect runtime provenance information. This component sends notifications back to users notifying them of events like failures, success, and completion of workflows and jobs.

The Pegasus software architecture includes also an error recovery system that attempts to recover from failures by retrying tasks or an entire workflow, remapping portions of the workflow, providing workflow-level checkpointing, and using alternative data sources, when possible. The Pegasus system records provenance information including the locations of data used and produced, and which software was used with which parameters. This feature is useful when a workflow must be reproduced.

## 4.1.2 Swift

Swift (Wilde et al., 2011) is a implicitly parallel scripting language that runs workflows across several distributed systems, like clusters, clouds, grids, and supercomputers. The Swift language has been designed at the University of Chicago and at the Argonne National Lab to provide users with a workflow-based language for grid computing. Recently it has been ported on clouds and exascale systems.

Swift separates the application workflow logic from the runtime configuration. This approach results in a flexible development model. As the DMCF programming interface, the Swift language allows invocation and running of external application code and allows binding with application execution environments without extra coding from the user. Swift/K is the previous version of the Swift language that runs on the Karajan grid workflow engine across wide-area resources. Swift/T is a new implementation of the Swift language for high-performance computing. In this implementation, a Swift program is translated into an MPI program that uses the Turbine and ADLB runtime libraries for scalable dataflow processing over MPI. The Swift-Turbine Compiler (STC) is an optimizing compiler for Swift/T and the Swift Turbine runtime is a distributed engine that maps the load of Swift workflow tasks across multiple computing nodes. Users can also use Galaxy (Giardine et al., 2005) to provide a visual interface for Swift.

The Swift language provides a functional programming paradigm where workflows are designed as a set of code invocations with their associated command-line arguments and input and output files. Swift is based on a C-like syntax and uses an implicit data-driven task parallelism (Wozniak et al., 2014). In fact, it looks like a sequential language, but being a dataflow language, all variables are *futures*, thus execution is based on data availability. When input data is ready, functions are executed in parallel. Moreover, parallelism can be exploited through the use of the *foreach* statement. The Turbine runtime comprises a set of services that implement the parallel execution of Swift scripts exploiting the maximal concurrency permitted by data dependencies within a script and by external resource availability. Swift has been used for developing several scientific data analysis applications, such as prediction of protein structures, modeling the molecular structure of new materials, and decision making in climate and energy policy. A programming example written in Swift is discussed in Section 4.4.4.

### 4.1.3 Hunk

Hunk is a commercial data analysis platform developed by Splunk for rapidly exploring, analyzing, and visualizing data in Hadoop and NoSQL data stores. Hunk uses a set of high-level user and programming interfaces to offer speed and simplicity of getting insights from large unstructured and structured datasets. One of the key components of the Hunk architecture is the Splunk Virtual Index. This system decouples the storage tier from the data access and analytics tiers, so enabling Hunk to route requests to different data stores. The analytics tier is based on Splunk's Search Processing Language (SPL) designed for data exploration across large, different datasets.

The Hunk web framework allows building applications on top of the Hadoop Distributed File System (HDFS) and/or the NoSQL data store. Developers can use Hunk to build their big data applications on top of data in Hadoop using a set of well-known languages and frameworks. Indeed, the framework enables developers to integrate data and functionality from Hunk into enterprise big data applications using a web framework, documented REST API and software development kits for C#, Java, JavaScript, PHP, and Ruby. Developers can use common development languages such as HTML5 and Python.

The Hunk framework can be deployed on on-premises Hadoop clusters or private clouds and is available as a preconfigured instance on the Amazon public cloud using the Amazon Web Services (AWS). This public cloud solution allows Hunk users to utilize the Hunk facilities and tools from AWS, also exploiting commodity storage on Amazon S3, according to a pay-per-use model. Finally, the framework implements and makes available a set of applications that enable the Hunk analytics platform to explore and visualize data in NoSQL and other data stores, including Apache Accumulo, Apache Cassandra, MongoDB and Neo4j. Hunk is also provided in combination with the Cloudera's enterprise data hub to develop large-scale applications that can access and analyze big datasets.

## 4.1.4 Sector/Sphere

Sector/Sphere is a cloud framework designed at the University of Illinois-Chicago to implement data analysis applications involving large, geographically distributed datasets in which the data can be naturally processed in parallel (Gu and Grossman, 2009). The framework includes two components: a storage service called *Sector*, which manages the large distributed datasets with high reliability, high-performance IO, and a uniform access, and a compute service called *Sphere*, which makes use of the Sector service to simplify data access, increase data IO bandwidth, and exploit wide-area high-performance networks. Both of them are available as open source software.[1]

Sector is a distributed storage system that can be deployed over a wide area and allows users to ingest and download large datasets from any location with a high-speed network connection to the system. The system can be deployed over a large number of commodity computers (called nodes), located either within a data center or across data centers, which are connected by high-speed networks. In an example scenario, nodes in the same rack are connected by 1 Gbps networks, two racks in the same data center are connected by 10 Gbps networks, and two different data centers are connected by 10 Gbps networks. Sector assumes that the datasets it stores are divided into one or more separate files, called *slices*, which are replicated and distributed over the various nodes managed by Sector.

---

http://sector.sourceforge.net

The Sector architecture includes a *Security server*, a *Master server*, and a number of *Slave nodes*. The Security server maintains user accounts, file access information, and the list of authorized slave nodes. The Master server maintains the metadata of the files stored in the system, controls the running of the slave nodes, and responds to users' requests. The Slaves nodes store the files managed by the system and process the data upon the request of a Sector client.

Sphere is a compute service built on top of Sector and provides a set of programming interfaces to write distributed data analysis applications. Sphere takes streams as inputs and produces streams as outputs. A stream consists of multiple data segments that are processed by Sphere Processing Engines (SPEs) using slave nodes. Usually there are many more segments than SPEs. Each SPE takes a segment from a stream as an input and produces a segment of a stream as output. These output segments can in turn be the input segments of another Sphere process. Developers can use the Sphere client APIs to initialize input streams, upload processing function libraries, start Sphere processes, and read the processing results.

### 4.1.5 BigML

BigML[2] is provided as a Software-as-a-Service (SaaS) for discovering predictive models from data sources and using data classification and regression algorithms. The distinctive feature of BigML is that predictive models are presented to users as interactive decision trees. The decision trees can be dynamically visualized and explored within the BigML interface, downloaded for local usage and/or integration with applications, services, and other data analysis tools. Extracting and using predictive models in BigML consists of multiple steps, as detailed in the following:

- *Data source setting and dataset creation*: A data source is the raw data from which a user wants to extract a predictive model. Each data source instance is described by a set of columns, each one representing an instance feature, or field. One of the fields is considered as the feature to be predicted. A dataset is created as a structured version of a data source in which each field has been processed and serialized according to its type (numeric, categorical, etc.).

---

[2]https://bigml.com

- *Model extraction and visualization*: Given a dataset, the system generates the number of predictive models specified by the user, who can also choose the level of parallelism level for the task. The interface provides a visual tree representation of each predictive model, allowing users to adjust the support and confidence values and to observe in real time how these values influence the model.

- *Prediction making*: A model can be used individually, or in a group (the so-called ensemble, composed of multiple models extracted from different parts of a dataset), to make predictions on new data. The system provides interactive forms to submit a predictive query for a new data using the input fields from a model or ensemble. The system provides APIs to automate the generation of predictions, which is particularly useful when the number of input fields is high.

- *Models evaluation*: BigML provides functionalities to evaluate the goodness of the predictive models extracted. This is done by generating performance measures that can be applied to the kind of extracted model (classification or regression).

## 4.1.6  Kognitio Analytical Platform

Kognitio Analytical Platform, available as cloud-based service or supplied as a preintegrated appliance, allows users to pull very large amounts of data from existing data storage systems into high-speed computer memory, allowing complex analytical questions to be answered interactively.[3]

Although Kognitio has its own internal disk subsystem, it is primarily used as an analytical layer on top of existing storage/data processing systems, for example, Hadoop clusters and/or existing traditional disk-based data warehouse products, cloud storage, etc. A feature called External Tables allows persistent data to reside on external systems. Using this feature the system administrator, or a privileged user, can easily setup access to data that resides in another environment, typically a disk store such as the above-mentioned Hadoop clusters and data warehouse systems.

To a final user, the Kognitio Analytical Platform looks like a relational database management system (RDBMS) similar to many commercial

www.kognitio.com

databases. However, unlike these databases, Kognitio has been designed specifically to handle analytical query workload, as opposed to the more traditional on-line transaction processing (OLTP) workload. Key reasons of Kognitio's high performance in managing analytical query workload are:

- Data is held in high-speed RAM using structures optimized for in-memory analysis, which is different from a simple copy of disk-based data, like a traditional cache.
- Massively Parallel Processing (MPP) allows scaling out across large arrays of low-cost industry standard servers, up to thousand nodes.
- Query parallelization allows every processor core on every server to be equally involved in every query.
- Machine code generation and advanced query plan optimization techniques ensure every processor cycle is effectively used to its maximum capacity.

Parallelism in Kognitio Analytical Platform fully exploits the so-called "shared nothing" distributed computing approach, in which none of the nodes share memory or disk storage, and there is no single point of contention across the system.

## 4.1.7 Mahout

Apache Mahout is an open-source framework that provides scalable implementations of machine learning algorithms. The goal of this project is to provide implementations of common machine learning algorithms applicable on big input in a scalable manner. The algorithms and techniques provided by Mahout can be divided in three main categories[4]: collaborative filtering, classification and clustering. In the following, some examples for each algorithm's category are listed: analyzing user history and preferences to suggest accurate recommendations (collaborative filtering), selecting whether a new input matches a previously observed pattern or not (classification), and grouping large number of things together into clusters that share some similarity (clustering) (Anil et al., 2012). Moreover, Mahout provides common algorithms for manipulating collections of data and for math operations (e.g., linear algebra and statistics).

---

[4]http://mahout.apache.org/users/basics/algorithms.html

Originally, the Mahout project provided implementations of machine learning algorithms executable on the top of Apache Hadoop framework. But the comparison of the performance of Mahout algorithms on Hadoop with other machine learning libraries, showed that Hadoop spends the majority of the processing time to load the state from file at every intermediate step (i.e., intermediate data are always stored in distributed file systems) (Shahrivari, 2014). For this reason, the Mahout project has recently supported algorithm implementations on other frameworks that are more suitable for machine learning such as Apache Spark and H20.[5] Both Apache Spark and H20 process data in memory so they can achieve a significant performance gain when compared to Hadoop framework for specific classes of applications (e.g., interactive jobs, real-time queries, and stream data) (Shahrivari, 2014).

## 4.1.8 Spark

Spark[6] is an open-source framework for in-memory data analysis and machine learning developed at UC Berkeley in 2009. It can process distributed data from several sources, such as HDFS, HBase, Cassandra, and Hive. It has been designed to efficiently perform both batch processing applications (similar to MapReduce) and dynamic applications like streaming, interactive queries, and graph analysis. Spark is compatible with Hadoop data and can run in Hadoop clusters through the YARN module. However, in contrast to Hadoop's two-stage MapReduce paradigm in which intermediate data are always stored in distributed file systems, Spark stores data in a cluster's memory and queries it repeatedly so as to obtain better performance for applications involving interactive jobs, real-time queries, and other specific types of computation (Xin et al., 2013). The Spark project has different components:

• Spark Core contains the basic functionalities of the library such as for manipulating collections of data, memory management, interaction with distributed file systems, task scheduling, and fault recovery.

---

http://0xdata.com/
http://spark.apache.org

- Spark SQL provides API to query and manipulate structured data using standard SQL or Apache Hive variant of SQL.[7]
- Spark Streaming provides an API for manipulating streams of data.
- GraphX is a library for manipulating and analyzing big graphs.
- MLlib is a scalable machine learning library on top of Spark that implements many common machine learning and statistical algorithms.

Several big companies and organizations use Spark for big data analysis purpose[8]: for example, Ebay[9] uses Spark for log transaction aggregation and analytics, Kelkoo[10] for product recommendations, SK Telecom[11] analyses mobile usage patterns of customers.

### 4.1.9 Microsoft Azure Machine Learning

Microsoft Azure Machine Learning (Azure ML) is a SaaS that provides a Web-based machine learning IDE (i.e., integrated development environment) for creation and automation of machine learning workflows. Through its user-friendly interface, data scientists and developers can perform several common data analysis/mining tasks on their data and automate their workflows.

Using its drag-and-drop interface, users can import their data in the environment or use special readers to retrieve data form several sources, such as Web URL (HTTP), OData Web service, Azure Blob Storage, Azure SQL Database, Azure Table. After that, users can compose their data analysis workflows where each data processing task is represented as a block that can be connected with each other through direct edges, establishing specific dependency relationships among them. Azure ML includes a rich catalog of processing tools that can be easily included in a workflow to prepare/transform data or to mine data through supervised learning (regression and classification) or unsupervised learning (clustering) algorithms. Optionally, users can include their own custom scripts (e.g., in R or Python) to extend the

---

[7]https://spark.apache.org/docs/1.1.0/sql-programming-guide.html
[8]http://cwiki.apache.org/confluence/display/SPARK/Powered+By+Spark
[9]http://www.ebay.com/
[10]http://www.kelkoo.com/
[11]http://www.sktelecom.com/

tools catalog. When workflows are correctly defined, users can evaluate them using some testing dataset. Users can easily visualize the results of the tests and find useful information about models accuracy, precision, and recall. Finally, in order to use their models to predict new data or perform real time predictions, users can expose them as Web services. Through a Web-based interface, users can monitor the Web services load and use over time.

Azure Machine Learning is a fully managed service provided by Microsoft on its cloud platform; users do not need to buy any hardware/software nor to manage virtual machines manually. One of the main advantages of working with a cloud platform like Azure is its auto-scaling feature: models are deployed as elastic Web services so that users do not have to worry about scaling them if models usage increases.

## 4.1.10  ClowdFlows

ClowdFlows (Kranjc et al., 2012) is an open source cloud-based platform for the composition, execution, and sharing of data analysis workflows. It is provided as a software as a service that allows users to design and execute visual workflows through a simple Web browser and so it can be run from most devices (e.g., desktop PCs, laptops, and tablets).

ClowdFlows is based on two software components: the workflow editor (provided by a Web browser) and the server side application that manages the execution of the application workflows and hosts a set of stored workflows. The server side consists of methods for supporting the client-side workflow editor in the composition and for executing workflows, and a relational database of workflows and data.

The workflow editor includes a workflow canvas and a widget repository. The widget repository is a list of all the available workflow components that can be added to the workflow canvas. The repository includes a set of default widgets. According to this approach, the CloudFlows service-oriented architecture allows users to include in their workflow the implementations of various algorithms, tools and Web services as workflow elements. For example, the Weka's algorithms have been included and exposed as Web services and so they can be added in a workflow application.

ClowdFlows is also easily extensible by importing third-party Web services that wrap open-source or custom data mining algorithms. To this end, a user has only to insert the WSDL URL of a Web service to create a new workflow element that represents the Web service in a workflow application.

## 4.2  HOW TO DESIGN A SCALABLE DATA ANALYSIS FRAMEWORK IN CLOUDS

As we discussed, designing and executing data analysis workflows over cloud platforms requires the availability of effective programming environments and efficient runtime systems. According to this observation, we designed and prototyped the Data Mining Cloud Framework (DMCF), a programming and runtime system for enabling the scalable execution of complex data analysis workflows on clouds. DMCF provides visual and script-based programming interfaces that allow developers to model complex data analysis workflows without worrying about low-level aspects that can be addressed by the runtime system or the cloud platform. In addition, the DMCF's runtime fully exploits the underlying cloud infrastructure enabling workflow execution on multiple virtual machines, this way reducing the turnaround times of complex data analysis workflows.

DMCF functionality is provided according with the SaaS model. This means that no installation is required on the user's machine: the DMCF visual user interface works in any modern Web browser, and so it can be invoked from most devices, including desktop PCs, laptops, and tablets. This is a key feature for users who need ubiquitous and seamless access to scalable data analysis services, without having to cope with installation and system management issues. A distinctive feature of DMCF is that it has been designed to run on top of a Platform-as-a-Service (PaaS) cloud. An important advantage of this approach is the independence from the infrastructure layer. In fact, the DMCF's components are mapped into PaaS services, which in turn are implemented on infrastructure components. Possible changes to the cloud infrastructure affect only the infrastructure/platform interface, which is managed by the cloud provider, and therefore DMCF's implementation and functionality are not influenced. In addition, the

PaaS approach facilitates the implementation of the system on a public cloud, which free final users and organizations from any hardware and OS management duties.

Another key feature of DMCF is the provision of novel data mining-specific workflow formalisms (Data and Tool arrays) that significantly ease the design of parallel and distributed data analysis applications. A Data array allows representing an ordered collection of input/output data sources in a single workflow node. Similarly, a Tool array node represents multiple instances of the same tool. Array nodes are effective to fork the concurrent execution of many parallel tasks to cloud resources, thus improving scalability.

### 4.2.1 Architecture and Execution Mechanisms

The architecture of DMCF includes different kinds of components that can be grouped into storage and compute components (see Figure 4.1).

The storage components include:

• *Data Folder*, which contains data sources and the results of data analysis processes, and *Tool Folder*, which contains libraries and executable files for data selection, preprocessing, transformation, data mining, and results evaluation.

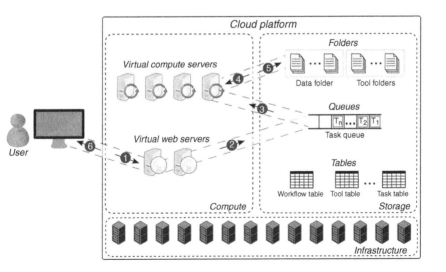

*Fig. 4.1. Architecture of the Data Mining Cloud Framework.*

- *Workflow Table, Tool Table* and *Task Table*, which contain metadata information associated with workflows, tools, and tasks.
- *Task Queue*, which contains the tasks ready for execution.

The compute components are:

- A pool of *Virtual Compute Servers*, which are in charge of executing the data analysis tasks.
- A pool of *Virtual Web Servers*, which host the Web-based user interface.

The user interface provides access to three functionalities: (i) *App submission*, which allows users to define and submit data analysis applications; (ii) *App monitoring*, which is used to monitor the status and access results of the submitted applications; (iii) *Data/Tool management*, which allows users to manage input/output data and tools.

Design and execution of a data analysis application in DMCF is a multistep process (see Figure 4.1):

1. The user accesses the Website and designs the workflow through a Web-based interface.
2. After workflow submission, the system creates a set of tasks and inserts them into the Task Queue.
3. Each idle Virtual Compute Server picks a task from the Task Queue, and concurrently executes it.
4. Each Virtual Compute Server gets the input dataset from its location. To this end, a file transfer is performed from the Data Folder where the dataset is located, to the local storage of the Virtual Compute Server.
5. After task completion, each Virtual Compute Server puts the result on the Data Folder.
6. The Website notifies the user whenever each task is completed, and allows her/him to access the results.

The set of tasks created on the second step depends on how many tools are invoked within the workflow. All the potential parallelism of the workflow is exploited by using the needed Virtual Compute Servers. In addition, multithreaded tasks exploit all the cores available on the Virtual Compute Servers they are assigned to.

## 4.2.2 Implementation on Microsoft Azure

A version of the Data Mining Cloud Framework has been implemented using Microsoft Azure, whose components and features have been introduced in Chapter 2. The choice of Azure was guided by the need of satisfying three main requirements:

- The use of a PaaS system, because implementing the execution mechanisms of DMCF does not require the low level facilities provided by a IaaS.
- The use of a platform whose components match the needs of the components defined in DMCF's architecture.
- The use of a public cloud, to free final users and organizations from any hardware and OS management duties.

Microsoft Azure satisfies all the requirements above, since it is a public PaaS platform whose components fully fit with those defined by DMCF. In the following, we describe how the generic components of DMCF's architecture are mapped to the Azure's components.

As shown in Figure 4.1, the architecture of DMCF distinguishes its high-level components into two groups, *Storage* and *Compute*, with the same approach followed by Azure and other cloud platforms. This made possible to implement the data and computing components of DMCF by fully exploiting the Storage and Compute components and functionalities provided by Azure.

For the Storage components, the following mapping with Azure was adopted:

1. Data Folder and Tool Folder are implemented as Azure's Blob containers;
2. Workflow Table, Tool Table, and Task Table, are implemented as nonrelational Tables;
3. Task Queue is implemented as an Azure's Queue.

For the Compute components, the following mapping was adopted:

1. Virtual Compute Servers are implemented as Worker Role instances;
2. Virtual Web Servers are implemented as Web Role instances.

Each Worker Role instance executes the operations described in Figure 4.2.

```
while true do
    if TaskQueue.isNotEmpty() then
        task ← TaskQueue.getTask();
        TaskTable.update(task, 'running');
        localInput = <local input location>;
        localOutput = <local output location>;
        transfer(task.input, localInput);
        taskStatus ← execute(task.algorithm, task.paramaters, localInput, localOutput);
        if taskStatus = 'done' then
            transfer(localOutput, task.outputBlobURI);
            TaskTable.update(task, 'done');
        end
        else
            TaskTable.update(task, 'failed');
        end
        TaskQueue.remove(task);
        delete(localInput);
        delete(localOutput);
    end
end
```

Fig. 4.2.   Pseudocode of the operations performed by each Worker Role instance in DMCF.

As shown by the algorithm, file transfers are performed when input/
output data have to be moved between storage and servers. To reduce
the impact of data transfer on the overall execution time, DMCF exploits the Azure's Affinity Group feature, which allows Data Folder and
Virtual Compute Servers to be located near to each other in the same
data center for optimal performance. At least one Virtual Web Server
runs continuously in the cloud, as it serves as user front-end for DMCF.
Moreover, the user indicates the minimum and maximum number of
Virtual Compute Servers he/she wants to use. DMCF exploits the auto-
scaling features of Microsoft Azure that allows spinning up or shutting
down Virtual Compute Servers, based on the number of tasks ready for
execution in the DMCFs Task Queue.

## 4.3  PROGRAMMING WORKFLOW-BASED DATA ANALYSIS

Workflows may encompass all the steps of discovery based on the execution of complex algorithms and the access and analysis of scientific data.
In data-driven discovery processes, knowledge discovery workflows can
produce results that can confirm real experiments or provide insights
that cannot be achieved in laboratories. In particular, DMCF allows
users to program workflow applications using two languages (Marozzo
et al., 2015):

- *VL4Cloud* (Visual Language for Cloud), a visual programming language that lets users develop applications by programming the workflow components graphically.
- *JS4Cloud* (JavaScript for Cloud), a scripting language for programming data analysis workflows based on JavaScript.

Both languages use two key programming abstractions:

- *Data* elements denote input files or storage elements (e.g., a dataset to be analyzed) or output files or stored elements (e.g., a data mining model).
- *Tool* elements denote algorithms, software tools or complex applications performing any kind of operation that can be executed on a data element (data mining, filtering, partitioning, etc.).

A descriptor, expressed in JSON format, is associated with each Data and Tool element. A Tool descriptor includes a reference to its executable, the required libraries, and the list of input and output parameters. Each parameter is characterized by name, description, type, and can be mandatory or optional. An example of descriptor for a data classification tool is presented in Figure 4.3.

The JSON descriptor of a new tool is automatically created through a guided procedure provided by DMCF, which allows users to specify all

```
"J48": {
   "libraryList": ["java.exe","weka.jar"],
   "executable": "java.exe -cp weka.jar weka.classifiers.trees.J48",
   "parameterList":[{
       "name": "dataset", "flag": "-t",
       "mandatory": true, "parType": "IN",
       "type": "file", "array": false,
       "description": "Input dataset"
   },{
       "name": "confidence", "flag": "-C",
       "mandatory": false, "parType": "OP",
       "type": "real", "array": false,
       "description": "Confidence value",
       "value": "0.25"
   },{
       "name": "model", "flag": "-d",
       "mandatory": true, "parType": "OUT",
       "type": "file", "array": false,
       "description": "Output model"}]}
```

*Fig. 4.3. Example of a tool descriptor in JSON format.*

the needed information for invoking the tool (executable, input and output parameters, etc.). A DMCF module, called Tool Manager, supports the deployment of new tools in the system allowing their subsequent use in DMCF's workflows. To this end, the Tool Manager performs the following tasks:

1. uploads libraries and executable files in Tool Folder;
2. creates a tool descriptor in JSON format;
3. publishes the JSON descriptor in Tool Table.

Similarly, a Data descriptor contains information to access an input or output file, including its identifier, location, and format. Differently from Tool descriptors, Data descriptors can also be created dynamically as a result of a task operation during the execution of a workflow. For example, if a workflow $W$ reads a dataset $D_i$ and creates (writes) a new dataset $D_j$, only $D_i$'s descriptor will be present in the environment before $W$'s execution, whereas $D_j$'s descriptor will be created at runtime.

Another common element is the *task* concept, which represents the unit of parallelism in the DMCF model. A task is a Tool invoked in the workflow, which is intended to run in parallel with other tasks on a set of cloud resources. According to this approach, VL4Cloud and JS4Cloud implement a *data-driven task parallelism*. This means that, as soon as a task does not depend on any other task in the same workflow, the runtime asynchronously spawns it to the first available virtual machine. A task $T_j$ does not depend on a task $T_i$ belonging to the same workflow (with $i \neq j$), if $T_j$ during its execution does not read any data element created by $T_i$.

### 4.3.1 VL4Cloud

In *VL4Cloud*, workflows are directed acyclic graphs whose nodes represent data and tools elements. The nodes can be connected with each other through direct edges, establishing specific dependency relationships among them. When an edge is being created between two nodes, a label is automatically attached to it representing the type of relationship between the two nodes.

For example, Figure 4.4 shows a J48 Tool (an implementation of the C4.5 algorithm (Quinlan, 1993) provided by the Weka toolkit (Hall et al., 2009)) that takes in input a TrainSet and generates a Model

Fig. 4.4. Example of a tool connected to input dataset and output model.

For each Tool node, input/output connections are allowed on the basis of the Tool descriptor present in Tool Table.

Data and Tool nodes can be added to the workflow as single instances or in an array form. A data array is an ordered collection of input/output data elements, while a tool array represents multiple instances of the same tool.

In order to present the main features of VL4Cloud, we use as an example a data analysis application composed of several sequential and parallel steps. The example application analyzes a dataset by using *n* instances of the J48 classification algorithm that work on *n* partitions of the training set and generate *n* classification models. By using the *n* generated models and the test set, *n* predictors produce in parallel *n* classified datasets. In the final step of the workflow, a voter generates the final classification by assigning a class to each data item. This is done by choosing the class predicted by the majority of the models (Zhou and Li, 2010).

Figure 4.5a shows a snapshot of the visual interface with the first step of the workflow, where the original dataset is split in training and test set by a partitioning tool. Since a set of parameters is associated with each workflow node, the interface allows users to configure them through a pop-up panel. For example, the central part of Figure 4.5a shows the configuration panel for the partitioning tool. In this case, only one parameter can be specified, namely which percentage of the input dataset must be used as training set. In a second step, the training set is partitioned into 16 parts using another partitioning tool (see Figure 4.5b). The 16 training sets resulting from the partitioning are represented in the workflow as a single data array node, labeled as Train-SetPart[16]. Figure 4.5c shows the third step of the workflow, in which the 16 training sets are analyzed in parallel by 16 instances of the J48 classification algorithm, to produce the same number of classification

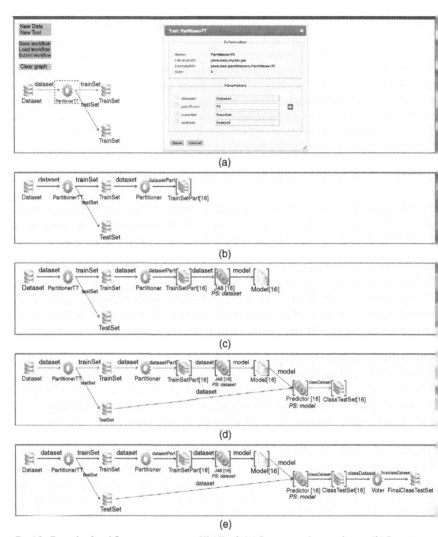

Fig. 4.5. Example of workflow composition using VL4Cloud. (a) Partitioning the input dataset. (b) Partitioning the train set. (c) Analyzing each train set part. (d) Classifying the test set. (e) Voting.

models. A tool array node, labeled as J48[16], is used to represent the 16 instances of the J48 algorithm, while another data array node, labeled as Model[16], represents the models generated by the classification algorithms. In practice, this part of the workflow specifies that J48[i] takes in input TrainSetPart[i] to produce Model[i], for $1 \leq i \leq 16$. The fourth step classifies the test set using the 16 models generated on the previous step (see Figure 4.5d). The classification is performed by 16 predictors that run in parallel to produce 16 classified test sets. In

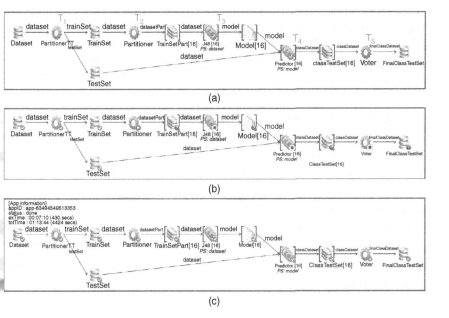

Fig. 4.6. Execution of the VL4Cloud workflow shown in Figure 4.5. (a) Workflow tasks. (b) Workflow running. (c) Workflow completed.

more detail, Predictor[i] takes in input TestSet and Model[i] to produce ClassTestSet[i], for 1 ≤ i ≤ 16. Finally, the 16 classified test sets are passed to a voter that produces the final dataset, labeled as FinalClassTestSet (see Figure 4.5e).

When the workflow design is complete, execution proceeds as detailed in the following. The five tools (PartitionerTT, Partitioner, J48, Predictor, and Voter) are translated into five groups of tasks, indicated as T1...T5 in Figure 4.6a.

The execution order of the workflow tasks depends on the dependencies specified by the workflow edges. To ensure the correct execution order, to each task is associated a list of tasks that must be completed before starting its execution. Figure 4.7 shows a possible order in which

| $T_5$ | $T_{4[16]}$ | ... | $T_{4[1]}$ | $T_{3[16]}$ | ... | $T_{3[1]}$ | $T_2$ | $T_1$ |
|---|---|---|---|---|---|---|---|---|
| $<T_{4[1]}, ...T_{4[16]}>$ | $<T_1, T_{3[16]}>$ | ... | $<T_1, T_{3[1]}>$ | $<T_2>$ | ... | $<T_2>$ | $<T_1>$ | $<>$ |

Fig. 4.7. A possible order in which the tasks are inserted into TaskQueue.

the tasks are generated and inserted into TaskQueue. For each task, the list of tasks to be completed before its execution is included. Note that task group T3, which represents the execution of 16 instances of J48, is translated into 16 tasks T3[1]...T3[16]. Similarly, T4 is translated into tasks T4[1]...T4[16].

According with the tasks dependencies specified by the workflow, the execution of T2 will start after completion of T1. As soon as T2 completes, the 16 tasks that compose T3 can be run concurrently. Each task T4[i] can be executed only after completion of both T2 and T3[i], for $1 \le i \le 16$. Finally T5 will start after completion of all tasks that compose T4. Figure 4.6b shows a snapshot of the workflow taken during its execution. The figure shows that PartitionerTT has completed the execution, Partitioner is running, while the other tools are still submitted. Figure 4.6c shows the workflow after completion of its execution. Some statistics about the overall application are shown on the upper left part of the window. In this example, it is shown that, using 16 virtual machines, the workflow completed 430 s after its submission, whereas the total execution time (i.e., the sum of the execution times of all the tasks) is 4424 s.

### 4.3.2 JS4Cloud

In *JS4Cloud*, workflows are defined through a JavaScript code that interacts with Data and Tool elements by three sets of functions, listed in Table 4.1:

- *Data Access*: for accessing a Data element stored in the cloud;
- *Data Definition*: to define a new Data element that will be created at runtime as a result of a Tool execution;
- *Tool Execution*: to invoke the execution of a Tool available in the cloud.

Data Access is implemented by the Data.get function, which is available in two versions: the first one receives the name of a data element and returns a reference to it. The second one returns an array of references to the data elements whose name matches the provided regular expression. For example, the following statement:

```
var ref = Data.get ("Census");
```

**Table 4.1  JS4Cloud Functions**

| Functionality | Function | Description |
|---|---|---|
| Data Access | Data.get(*<dataName>*); | Returns a reference to the data element with the provided name. |
| | Data.get(new RegExp(*<regular expression>*)); | Returns an array of references to the data elements whose name match the regular expression. |
| Data Definition | Data.define(*<dataName>*); | Defines a new data element that will be created at runtime. |
| | Data.define(*<arrayName>*,*<dim>*); | Define an array of data elements. |
| | Data.define(*<arrayName>*,[*<dim$_1$>*,...,*<dim$_n$>*]); | Define a multi-dimensional array of data elements. |
| Tool Execution | *<toolName>*({*<par$_1$>*:*<val$_1$>*,...,*<par$_n$>*:*<val$_n$>*}); | Invokes an existing tool with associated parameter values. |

assigns to variable `ref` a reference to the dataset named `Census`, while the following statement:

```
var ref = Data.get(new RegExp("^CensusPart"));
```

assigns to `ref` an array of references (`ref[0]...ref[n-1]`) to all the datasets whose name begins with `CensusPart`.

Data Definition is done through the `Data.define` function, available in three versions: the first one defines a single data element; the second one defines a one-dimensional array of data elements; the third one defines a multidimensional array of data elements. For instance, the following piece of code:

```
var ref = Data.define("CensusModel");
```

defines a new data element named `CensusModel` and assigns its reference to variable `ref`, while the following statement:

```
var ref = Data.define("CensusModel", 16);
```

defines an array of data elements of size 16 (`ref[0]...ref[15]`).

The following is an example statement defining a bidimensional array of data elements of size 4 times 16:

```
var ref = Data.define("ClassDataset", [4,16]);
```

In all cases, the data elements defined using `Data.define` will be created at runtime as result of a tool execution.

Differently from Data Access and Data Definition, there is not a named function for Tool Execution. In fact, the invocation of a tool T is made by calling a function with the same name of T. The DMCF makes the tools available to the users by loading their descriptions into the environment. For example, the J48 tool defined by the descriptor in Figure 4.3 can be invoked as in the following statement:

```
J48({dataset:DRef, confidence:0.05, model:MRef});
```

where DRef is a reference to the dataset to be analyzed, previously introduced using the `Data.get` function, and MRef is a reference to the model to be generated, previously introduced using `Data.define`.

From an implementation perspective, the `Data.get` primitive returns a reference to a data element stored in Data Folder, which is a persistent storage independent from the local storage of each Virtual Compute Server. Whenever a data element referenced by `Data.get` must be processed, it is transparently copied to the local storage of the virtual server onto which processing will take place. Similarly, the `Data.define` primitive defines a new data element that will be created at runtime in the local storage of a virtual server, as a consequence of a tool execution. The data elements created in such a way are then transparently copied to the Data Folder.

Figure 4.8 shows the JS4Cloud workflow corresponding to VL4Cloud workflow shown in Figure 4.5. Parallelism is exploited in the for loop at line 7, where up to 16 instances of the J48 classifier are executed in parallel on 16 different partitions of the training set, and in the for loop at line 10, where up to 16 instances of the Predictor are executed in parallel to classify the test set using 16 different classification models.

The DMCF interface allows users to monitor the execution of JS4Cloud scripts. To this end, beside each code line number, a colored circle indicates the status of execution. A green circle indicates that the tasks on a given line have completed their execution; blue circle.

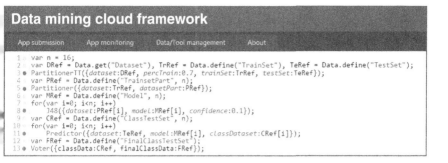

```
Data mining cloud framework

App submission    App monitoring    Data/Tool management    About

 1   var n = 16;
 2   var DRef = Data.get("Dataset"), TrRef = Data.define("TrainSet"), TeRef = Data.define("TestSet");
 3 ● PartitionerTT({dataset:DRef, percTrain:0.7, trainSet:TrRef, testSet:TeRef});
 4   var PRef = Data.define("TrainsetPart", n);
 5 ● Partitioner({dataset:TrRef, datasetPart:PRef});
 6   var MRef = Data.define("Model", n);
 7   for(var i=0; i<n; i++)
 8 ●     J48({dataset:PRef[i], model:MRef[i], confidence:0.1});
 9   var CRef = Data.define("ClassTestSet", n);
10   for(var i=0; i<n; i++)
11 ●     Predictor({dataset:TeRef, model:MRef[i], classDataset:CRef[i]});
12   var FRef = Data.define("FinalClassTestSet");
13 ● Voter({classData:CRef, finalClassData:FRef});
```

*Fig. 4.8.   JS4Cloud workflow corresponding to the VL4Cloud workflow shown in Figure 4.5.*

denote tasks that are still running; orange circles denote tasks that are waiting to be executed.

### 4.3.3 Workflow Patterns in DMCF

In the following we describe how the basic control flow patterns can be programmed with VL4Cloud and JS4Cloud. We focus on basic patterns (Bharathi et al., 2008) such as *single task*, *pipeline*, *data partitioning* and *data aggregation*, and on three additional patterns supported by DMCF, namely *parameter sweeping*, *input sweeping*, and *tool sweeping*. For each pattern, we first introduce an example as a VL4Cloud workflow, and then we show how the same example can be coded using JS4Cloud.

#### 4.3.3.1 Single Task

An example of single-task pattern is shown in the following figure:

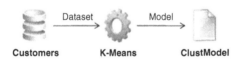

This example represents a K-Means tool that produces a clustering model from the Customers dataset. In this example, a configuration parameter that has been set by the user, for example, the number of clusters for the K-Means tool, is not visible. The following JS4Cloud script is equivalent to the visual workflow shown above:

```
var DRef = Data.get ("Customers");
```

```
var nc = 5;

var MRef = Data.define("ClustModel");

K-Means({dataset:DRef, numClusters:nc, model:MRef});
```

The script accesses the dataset to be analyzed (Customers), sets to five the number of clusters, and defines the name of data element that will contain the clustering model (ClustModel). Then, the K-Means tool is invoked along with the parameters indicated in its JSON descriptor (input dataset, number of clusters, output model).

### 4.3.3.2 Pipeline
In the pipeline pattern, the output of a task is the input for the subsequent task, as in the following example:

The first part of the shown example extracts a sample from an input dataset using a tool named Sampler. The second part creates a classification model from the sample using the J48 tool. This pattern example is implemented in JS4Cloud as follows:

```
var DRef = Data.get("Census");

var SDRef = Data.define("SCensus");

Sampler({input:DRef, percent:0.25, output:SDRef});

var MRef = Data.define("CensusTree");

J48({dataset:SDRef, confidence:0.1, model:MRef});
```

In this case, since J48 receives as input the output of Sampler, the former will be executed only after completion of the latter.

### 4.3.3.3 Data Partitioning
The data partitioning pattern produces two or more output data from an input data element, as in the following example:

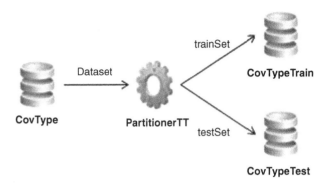

In this example a training set and a test set are extracted from a dataset, using a tool named `PartitionerTT`. With JS4Cloud, this can be written as follows:

```
var DRef = Data.get("CovType");

var TrRef = Data.define("CovTypeTrain");

var TeRef = Data.define("CovTypeTest");

PartitionerTT({dataset:DRef, percTrain:0.70, trainSet:TrRef,
    testSet:TeRef});
```

If data partitioning is used to divide a dataset into a number of splits, the DMCF's data array formalism can be conveniently used as in the following example:

In this case, a `Partitioner` tool splits a dataset into 16 parts. The corresponding JS4Cloud code is:

```
var DRef = Data.get("NetLog");

var PRef = Data.define("NetLogParts", 16);

Partitioner({dataset:DRef, datasetParts:PRef});
```

Note that an array of 16 data elements is first defined and then created by the `Partitioner` tool.

### 4.3.3.4 Data Aggregation
The data aggregation pattern generates one output data from multiple input data, as in the following example:

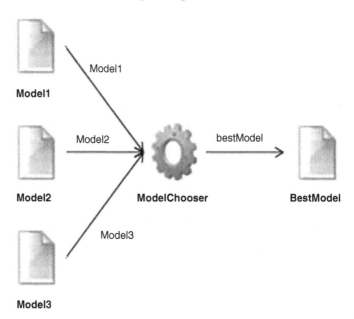

In this example, a `ModelChooser` tool takes as input three data mining models and chooses the best one based on some evaluation criteria. The corresponding JS4Cloud script is:

```
var M1Ref = Data.get("Model1");

var M2Ref = Data.get("Model2");

var M3Ref = Data.get("Model3");

var BMRef = Data.define("BestModel");

ModelChooser({model1:M1Ref, model2:M2Ref, model3:M3Ref,
    bestModel:BMRef});
```

DMCF's data arrays may be used for a more compact visual representation. For example, the following pattern example chooses the best one among 8 models:

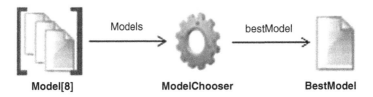

| Model[8] | ModelChooser | BestModel |

The same task can be coded as follows using JS4Cloud:

```
var BMRef = Data.define("BestModel");

ModelChooser({models:MsRef, bestModel:BMRef});
```

In this script, it is assumed that MsRef is a reference to an array of models created on a previous step.

### 4.3.3.5  Parameter Sweeping

Parameter sweeping is a data analysis pattern in which a dataset is analyzed in parallel by multiple instances of the same tool with different parameters, as in the following example:

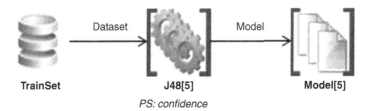

| TrainSet | J48[5] | Model[5] |

PS: confidence

In this example, a training set is processed in parallel by five instances of J48 to produce the same number of data mining models. The DM-CF's tool array formalism is used to represent the five tools in a compact form. The J48 instances differ from each other by the value of a single parameter, the confidence factor, which has been configured (through the visual interface) to range from 0.1 to 0.5 with a step of 0.1. The equivalent JS4Cloud script is:

```
var TRef = Data.get("TrainSet");

var nMod = 5;

var MRef = Data.define("Model", nMod);

var min = 0.1;
```

```
var max = 0.5;

for(var i = 0; i<nMod; i++)

    J48({dataset:TRef, model:MRef[i], confidence:
    (min + i*(max-min)/(nMod-1))});
```

In this case, the for loop is used to create five instances of J48, where the *i*th instance takes as input the same training set (TRef), and produces a different model (MRef[i]), using a specific value for the confidence parameter (0.1 for J48[0], 0.2 for J48[1], and so on). It is worth noticing that the tools are independent of each other, and so the runtime can execute them in parallel.

### 4.3.3.6 Input Sweeping
Input sweeping that exploits data parallelism is a pattern in which a set of input data is analyzed independently to produce the same number of output data. It is similar to the parameter-sweeping pattern, with the difference that in this case the sweeping is done on the input data rather than on a tool parameter. An example of input sweeping pattern is represented in the following figure:

In this example, 10 training sets are processed in parallel by 10 instances of J48, to produce the same number of data mining models. Data arrays are used to represent both input data and output models, while a tool array is used to represent the J48 tools. The following JS4Cloud script corresponds to the example shown above:

```
var nMod = 10;

var MRef = Data.define("Model", nMod);

for(var i = 0; i<nMod; i++)

    J48({dataset:TsRef[i], model:MRef[i], confidence:0.1});
```

It is assumed that TsRef is a reference to an array of training sets created on a previous step. The for loop creates 10 instances of J48, where the *i*th instance takes as input TsRef[i] to produce MRef[i].

Another example of input sweeping pattern is represented in the following figure:

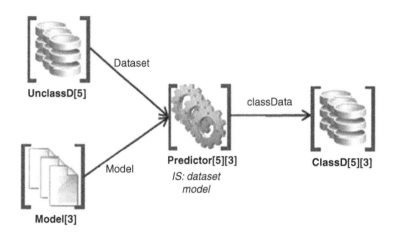

In this case there are 15 instances of a Predictor. Each Predictor takes as input one unclassified dataset and one model, and generates concurrently one classified dataset. The following JS4Cloud script corresponds to this example:

```
var nData = 5, nMod = 3;

var CRef = Data.define("ClassD", [nData, nMod]);

for(var i = 0; i<nData; i++)

   for(var j = 0; j<nMod; j++)

      Predictor({dataset:DRef[i], model:MRef[j],
         classDataset:CRef[i][j]});
```

Here is assumed that DRef is a reference to an array of unlabeled daasets, and MRef is a reference to an array of models, created on previous teps. The double for loop creates a bidimensional array of classified latasets, denoted CRef, where CRef[i][j] is the classified dataset generated by a Predictor instance on DRef[i] using MRef[j]. Also in this case, since the tools are independent of each other, they can be executed in parallel by the runtime.

### 4.3.3.7 Tool Sweeping

Tool sweeping is a pattern in which a dataset is analyzed in parallel by different tools, as in the following example:

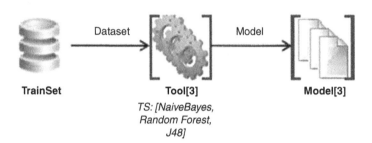

TrainSet    Tool[3]    Model[3]

TS: [NaiveBayes,
Random Forest,
J48]

In this example, each one of the three classification tools (Naive-Bayes, RandomForest, J48) analyzes the same training set to produce a classification model. The result of this pattern example are three different models. This corresponds to the following JS4Cloud script:

```
var TRef = Data.get("TrainSet");

var MRef = Data.define("Model", 3);

NaiveBayes({dataset:TRef, model:MRef[0],
    kernelDensity:true});

RandomForest({dataset:TRef, model:MRef[1],
    numberOfTrees:500});

J48({dataset:TRef, model:MRef[2], confidence:0.1});
```

### 4.3.3.8 Combination of Sweeping Patterns

In JS4Cloud, it is possible to combine parameter, input and tool sweeping patterns. In the following we show two examples of sweeping pattern combinations.

As a first example, we show an input/parameter sweeping, that is, the combination of input and parameter sweeping. With this pattern, each input data is analyzed in parallel by multiple instances of the same tool with different parameters, as in the following figure:

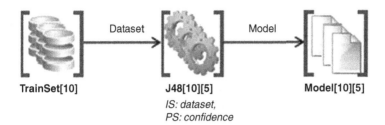

**TrainSet[10]**                **J48[10][5]**                **Model[10][5]**
                               *IS: dataset,*
                               *PS: confidence*

In this example, each of the 10 training sets is processed by five instances of J48 to produce five data mining models. Thus, there are in total 50 instances of J48, represented by a bidimensional array of size 10 times 5, that generate the same number of models. The following JS-4Cloud script corresponds to this example:

```
var nTr = 10;

var conf = [0.1, 0.2, 0.3, 0.4, 0.5];

var MRef = Data.define("Model", [nTr, conf.length]);

for(var i = 0; i<nTr; i++)

  for(var j = 0; j<conf.length; j++)

    J48({dataset:TsRef[i], model:MRef[i][j],
       confidence:conf[j]});
```

The second example is a tool/parameter sweeping, that is, the combination of tool and parameter sweeping. With this pattern, a dataset is analyzed in parallel by a set of tools, each of them configured with different parameters, as in the following figure:

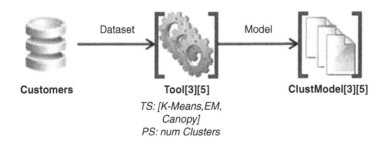

**Customers**                **Tool[3][5]**                **ClustModel[3][5]**
                            *TS: [K-Means,EM,*
                                *Canopy]*
                            *PS: num Clusters*

In this workflow, three clustering tools, K-Means, EM, and Canopy, analyze in parallel the same dataset. Each clustering algorithm is executed five times varying an algorithm parameter (the number of clusters). Thus, for each of the three clustering tools five instances are created. They are rerepresented by a bidimensional array of size 3 times 5. This is the equivalent JS4Cloud script:

```
var DRef = Data.get("Customers");

var nt = 3;

var nc = [3,4,5,6];

var MRef = Data.define("ClustModel", [nt, nc.length]);

for(var i = 0; i<nc.length; i++){

  K-Means({dataset:DRef, numClusters:nc[i],
    model:MRef[0,i]});

  EM({dataset:DRef, numClusters:nc[i], model:MRef[1,i]});

  Canopy({dataset:DRef, numClusters:nc[i],
    model:MRef[2,i]});

}
```

## 4.4 DATA ANALYSIS CASE STUDIES

In this section we describe four examples of data analysis workflows designed using some of the programming languages discussed in the previous sections, namely:

- a trajectory mining workflow designed using VL4Cloud;
- an ensemble learning workflow programmed with JS4Cloud;
- a data analysis workflow with MapReduce computations executed in DMCF;
- a parallel classification workflow programmed using Swift.

### 4.4.1 Trajectory Mining Workflow Using VL4Cloud

The increasing pervasiveness of mobile devices along with the use of technologies like GPS, Wi-fi networks, RFID, and sensors, allows fo

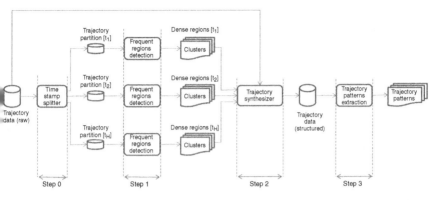

*Fig. 4.9.  Trajectory pattern mining abstract workflow.*

the collections of large amounts of movement data. This amount of information can be analyzed to extract descriptive and predictive models that can be properly exploited to improve urban life. Here we describe a workflow for discovering patterns and rules from trajectory data, designed using VL4Cloud and executed on DMCF (Altomare et al., 2014). In particular, the trajectory mining workflow described here analyzes the trajectories followed by mobile devices to catch users' mobility behaviors.

Figure 4.9 shows the trajectory pattern mining process, described through an abstract workflow formalism. The original dataset D is a raw trajectory data, populated by the trajectories (represented in the previously described format) of some users collected somehow. In particular, we assume that D is composed of N trajectories, each one represented as a sequence of $H$ $(x, y, t)$ triples. The workflow is composed of four steps, as described in the following:

- *Step 0 – Vertical Data Splitting*: D is partitioned vertically by a Time Stamp Splitter, based on the timestamp value. In other words, the points of the trajectories visited at time stamp $t_i \in T$ will be gathered in the $i$th output dataset. At the end of this step, |T| different datasets are available.

*Step 1 – Frequent Regions Detection*: This step is aimed at detecting, for each timestamp, the regions that are more densely visited compared to others (thus, of interest for the subsequent analysis). This is done by running H clustering algorithm instances, each one taking in input a dataset built at the previous step. The final result consists of $H$ clustering models, where the clusters of the $i$th model represent the dense regions of the $i$th time stamp (each cluster corresponds to a dense region). The number of detected regions (i.e., number of clusters) may be different for each timestamp.

- *Step 2 – Trajectory Data Synthetization*: This step is aimed at synthesizing the trajectories to build a structured trajectory dataset. This task is performed by running the Trajectory Synthesizer tool, whose goal is to create a dataset where each point of the original trajectories is substituted by the dense region it belongs to (discovered on Step 1). The final dataset, named Trajectory Data in figure, results populated by trajectories between dense regions.

- *Step 3 – Trajectory Pattern Extraction*: A Trajectory Pattern Extraction algorithm on the dense regions trajectory data is executed, to discover trajectory patterns from them. The final mining model is a set of associative rules describing spatio-temporal relations between the movement of the users under investigation.

Figure 4.10 shows a snapshot of the VL4Cloud workflow corresponding to the abstract workflow in Figure 4.9, executed on DMCF. The initial dataset, Trajectory Data, is partitioned into H subsets using the Time Stamp Splitter tool, where H = 128 is equal to the number of timestamps (Step 0). Then, each partition TrajPartition[i], is analyzed by an instance of DBScan and produces a ClusteringModel (Step 1). Each clustering model is a set of clusters/dense regions, for a given time stamp. The TrajectorySynthetizer tool analyzes all models and the initial

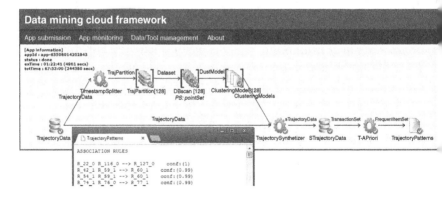

*Fig. 4.10. Execution of the VL4Cloud workflow corresponding to the abstract workflow shown in Figure 4.9.*

dataset, to generate the Structured Trajectory Data, where each point of the original trajectories is substituted by the dense region it belongs to (Step 2). Finally, T-APriori gets in input this dataset to extract trajectory patterns and, thus, produces the final results (Step 3).

The execution of the workflow using 64 cloud servers showed a significant reduction of turnaround time compared to that achieved by the sequential execution. In particular, the turnaround time passed from about 68 h using a single server, to about 1.4 h using 64 servers.

### 4.4.2 Ensemble Learning Workflow Using JS4Cloud

This workflow is the implementation of a multiclass cancer classifier based on the analysis of genes, using an ensemble learning approach (Kuncheva, 2004). The input dataset is the Global Cancer Map (GCM)[12], which contains the gene expression profiles of 280 samples representing 14 common human cancer classes. For each sample is reported the status of 16,063 genes and the type of tumor (class label). The GCM dataset is available as a training set containing 144 instances and as a test set containing 46 instances. The goal is to classify an unlabeled dataset (UnclassGCM) composed by 20,000 samples, divided in four parts.

The workflow begins by analyzing the training set using n instances of the J48 classification tool and m instances of the JRip classification tool (Weka's implementation of the Ripper [3] algorithm). The n J48 instances are obtained by sweeping the confidence and the minNumObj (minimum number of instances per leaf) parameters, while the m JRip instances are obtained by sweeping the numFolds (number of folders) and seed parameters. The resulting n + m classification models (classifiers) are passes as input to n + m evaluators, which produce an evaluation of each model against the test set. Then, k unclassified datasets are classified using the n + m models by k*(n + m) predictors. Finally, k voters take in input n + m model evaluations and the k*(n + m) classified datasets, producing k classified datasets through weighted voting. Figure 4.11 shows the JS4Cloud code of the workflow.

At the beginning, the training set is specified (line 1). Then, arrays conf and mno specify, respectively, the confidence and minNumObj values

---

http://eps.upo.es/bigs/datasets.html

```
 1: var TrRef = Data.get("GCM-train");
 2: var conf = [0.1, 0.25, 0.5], mno = [2, 5, 10], nfol = [3, 5, 10],
      snum = [1487, 5741, 7699];
 3: var n = conf.length*mno.length, m = nfol.length*snum.length;
 4: var M1Ref = Data.define("Model1", n), M2Ref = Data.define("Model2", m);
 5: for(var i=0; i<conf.length; i++)
 6:   for(var j=0; j<mno.length; j++)
 7:     J48({dataset:TrRef, model:M1Ref[i*mno.length+j], confidence:conf[i],
          minNumObj:mno[j]});
 8: for(var i=0; i<nfol.length; i++)
 9:   for(var j=0; j<snum.length; j++)
10:     JRip({dataset:TrRef, model:M2Ref[i*snum.length+j], numFolds:nfol[i],
          seed:snum[j]});
11: var TeRef = Data.get("GCM-test"), EvM1Ref = Data.define("EvModel1", n),
      EvM2Ref = Data.define("EvModel2", m);
12: for(var i=0; i<n; i++)
13:   Evaluator({dataset:TeRef, model:M1Ref[i], evalModel:EvM1Ref[i]});
14: for(var i=0; i<m; i++)
15:   Evaluator({dataset:TeRef, model:M2Ref[i], evalModel:EvM2Ref[i]});
16: var k = 4;
17: var DRef = Data.get("UnlabGCM", k), CRef = Data.define("ClassGCM",[k,n+m]);
18: for(var i=0; i<k; i++){
19:   for(var j=0; j<n; j++)
20:     Predictor({dataset:DRef[i], model:M1Ref[j], classDataset:CRef[i][j]});
21:   for(var j=0; j<m; j++)
22:     Predictor({dataset:DRef[i], model:M2Ref[j], classDataset:CRef[i][n+j]});
23: }
24: var FRef = Data.define("FinalClassGCM", k), EvMRef = EvM1Ref.concat(EvM2Ref);
25: for(var i=0; i<k; i++)
26:   WeightedVoter({classDataset:CRef[i], evalModel:EvMRef,
          finalClassDataset:FRef[i]});
```

*Fig. 4.11. Ensemble learning workflow programmed as a JS4Cloud script.*

for J48, while arrays nfol and snum specify, respectively, the numFolds and seed values for JRip (line 2). Given the size of the above arrays, variables n and m as defined on line 3 are both equal to 9. Afterwards, n instances of J48 and m instances of JRip are executed, where each instance uses a different combination of its parameters to analyze the training set (lines 5–10). Line 11 specifies the test set, which is used to evaluate the two arrays of models generated by the n J48 instances and the m JRip instances (lines 12–15). Then, k unlabeled datasets are specified as input with k = 4 (line 17). Each of the k input datasets is classified by n predictors using the n models generated by J48, and by m predictors using the m models generated by JRip; therefore, for each of the k input datasets, n + m classified datasets are generated (lines 18–23). As a final step, k weighted voters are executed; the *i*th voter receives the n + m classified datasets generated from the *i*th input and the n + m models, and return the final classified dataset for the *i*th input (lines 25–26). In general, the

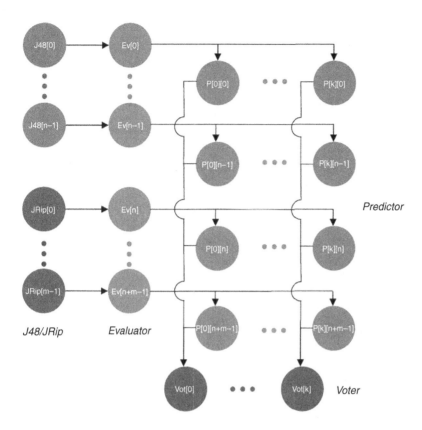

workflow is composed of $k + (k + 2)(n + m)$ tasks, which are related to each other as specified by the dependency graph shown in Figure 4.12.

In the specific example (with $n = 9$, $m = 9$, $k = 4$) the number of tasks is 112. As for the trajectory mining workflow introduced earlier, the cloud allowed us to speed up significantly the workflow execution. In fact, the turnaround time passed from about 162 min using a single server, to about 11 min using 19 servers, which results in a speedup of about 14.7.

## 4.4.3  Parallel Classification Using MapReduce in DMCF

In this section we describe a DMCF data classification workflow including MapReduce computations. Through this example, we show how the MapReduce paradigm can be integrated into VL4Cloud workflows, and how it can be used to exploit the inherent parallelism of the application. The application deals with a significant economic problem coupled with the flight delay prediction. Every year approximately 20% of airline flights are delayed or canceled mainly due to bad weather, carrier equipment, or technical airport problems. These delays result in significant cost to both airlines and passengers (Ball et al., 2010).

The goal of this application is to implement a predictor of the arrival delay of scheduled flights due to weather conditions. The predicted arrival delay takes into consideration both flight information (origin airport, destination airport, scheduled departure time, scheduled arrival time) and weather forecast at origin and destination airports. In particular, we consider the closest weather observation at origin and destination airports based on scheduled flight departure and arrival time. If the predicted arrival delay of a scheduled flight is less than a given threshold, it is classified as an on-time flight; otherwise, it is classified as a delayed flight.

Two open datasets of airline flights and weather observations have been collected, and exploratory data analysis has been performed to discover initial insights, evaluate the quality of data, and identify potentially interesting subsets. The first dataset is the *Airline On-Time Performance* (*AOTP*) provided by RITA - Bureau of Transportation Statistics.[13] The AOTP dataset contains data for domestic US flights by major air carriers, providing for each flight detailed information such as origin and destination airports, scheduled and actual departure and arrival times, air time, and nonstop distance. The second is the *Quality Controlled Local Climatological Data* (*QCLCD*) dataset available from the National Climatic Data Center.[14] The dataset contains hourly weather observations from about 1,600 US stations. Each weather observation includes data about temperature, humidity, wind direction and speed, barometric pressure, sky condition, visibility and weather phenomena descriptor.

For data classification, a MapReduce version of the Random Forest (RF) algorithm has been used. RF is an ensemble learning method for classification [13]. It creates a collection of different decision trees called *forest*. Once forest trees are created, the classification of an unlabeled

---

[13]http://www.transtats.bts.gov
[14]http://cdo.ncdc.noaa.gov/qclcd/QCLCD

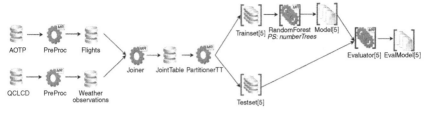

*Fig. 4.13.  Flight delay analysis workflow with MapReduce computations in DMCF.*

tuple is performed by aggregating the predictions of the different trees through majority voting.

Using DMCF, we created a VL4Cloud workflow for the whole data analysis process (see Figure 4.13). The workflow begins by preprocessing the AOTP and the QCLCD datasets using two instances of a PreProc Tool. These steps allow looking for possible wrong data, treating missing values, and filtering out diverted and cancelled flights and weather observations not related to airport locations. Then, a Joiner Tool executes a relational join between Flights and Weather Observations data in parallel using a MapReduce algorithm. The result is a JointTable. Then, a PartionerTT Tool creates five pairs <Trainset, Testset> using different delay threshold values. The five instances of training set and test set are represented in the workflow as two data array nodes, labelled as Trainset[5] and Testset[5].

Then, five instances of the RandomForest Tool analyze in parallel the ive instances of Trainset to generate five models (Model[5]). For each model, an instance of the Evaluator Tool generates the confusion matrix EvalModel), which is a commonly used method to measure the quality of classification. Starting from the set of confusion matrices obtained, hese tools calculate some metrics, e.g. accuracy, precision, recall, which an be used to select the best model.

To run the workflow, we deployed a Hadoop cluster composed of head node and 8 worker nodes, over the cloud servers used by the DMCF environment. With this setting, the turnaround time decreased rom about 7 h using 2 workers, to about 1.7 h using 8 workers, with a peedup that is very close to linear values. In this example, scalability is obtained exploiting the parallelism offered both by MapReduce Tools and by the VL4Cloud workflow language. In the first case, each MapRe-duce Tool is executed in parallel exploiting the cluster resources. The level of parallelism depends on the number of map and reduce tasks and on the resources available in the cluster. In the second case, VL4Cloud allows creating parallel paths and array of tools that can be executed concurrently. In this case, the parallelism level depends on the dependencies among tasks and on the resources available in the cluster.

### 4.4.4 Parallel Classification Using Swift

We describe here how the JS4Cloud workflow shown in Figure 4.8 can be coded using the Swift parallel scripting language. This application classifies a dataset by using *n* instances of the J48 classification algorithm that analyzes in parallel *n* partitions of the training set and generate *n* classification models. By using the *n* generated models and the test set, *n* predictor tasks generate in parallel *n* classified datasets. In the final step of the workflow, a voter generates the final classification by assigning a class to each data item. Choosing the class predicted by the majority of the models does this. For the reader's convenience, we report in Figure 4.14, the JS4Cloud code.

```
1   var n = 16;
2   var DRef = Data.get("Dataset"), TrRef = Data.define("TrainSet");
3   var TeRef = Data.define("TestSet");
4
5   PartitionerTT({dataset:DRef, percTrain:0.7, trainSet:TrRef,  testSet:TeRef})
6
7   var PRef = Data.define("TrainsetPart", n);
8
9   Partitioner({dataset:TrRef, datasetPart:PRef});
10
11  var MRef = Data.define("Model", n);
12
13  for(var i=0; i<n; i++)
14      J48({dataset:PRef[i], model:MRef[i], confidence:0.1});
15
16  var CRef = Data.define("ClassTestSet", n);
17
18  for(var i=0; i<n; i++)
19      Predictor({dataset:TeRef, model:MRef[i], classDataset:CRef[i]});
20
21  var FRef = Data.define("FinalClassTestSet");
22
23  Voter({classDataset:CRef, finalClassDataset:FRef});
```

*Fig. 4.14. JS4Cloud code of a parallel classification example.*

```
 1  type datafile {}
 2
 3  app (datafile output) J48 (datafile partition, int conf)
 4  {
 5     java.exe -cp weka.jar weka.classifiers.trees.j48 -t @partition -C @conf -d @output;
 6  }
 7  app (datafile output) Predictor (datafile test, datafile model)
 8  {...}
 9  app (datafile output) Voter (datafile[] classes)
10  {...}
11
12  int n = 16;
13  int perc = 70;
14  int confidence = 0.1;
15
15  datafile DRef <"Dataset">;
16  datafile TTRef[] <ext; exec = PartitionerTT, percTrain = perc; source = DRef>;
17  datafile PRef[]  <ext; exec = Partitioner; source = TTRef[0], n>;
18  datafile MRef[] <filesys_mapper; Prefix = "Model">;
19
20  foreach i in PRef {
21     MRef[i] = J48(PRef[i], confidence);
23  }
24  datafile CRef[] <filesys_mapper; Prefix = "ClassTestSet">;
25
26  foreach i in MRef {
27     CRef[i] = Predictor(TTRef[1], MRef[i]);
28  }
29  datafile FRef <"FinalClassTestSet">;
30  FRef = Voter(CRef);
```

*Fig. 4.15. Swift code of a parallel classification example.*

Swift is a scripting language that executes external programs in parallel. The Swift code in Figure 4.15 includes the definition of *mapped types* needed to declare the data elements that refer to files external to the Swift script (Wilde et al., 2011). These files can then be read and written by application programs called by Swift. Line 1 declares datafile type used for datsets. Lines 3–10 include the app declarations that in Swift describe how an external application program is invoked. Here are declared three application programs: the J48 classifier, the Predictor and the Voter. These declarations specify the application parameters and the program invocation string. Lines 12–14 declare program variables, line 15 declares the input dataset (Dataset) and lines 16–18, 24, and 29 declare the intermediate and output datasets. In particular, those declarations use mapping primitives (*mappers*) that make a given variable name refer to a filename. A mapper associated with a structured Swift variable can represent a large, structured dataset. Here are used built-in mappers (see lines 18 and 24) and external mappers (see lines 16–17) that include the reference to the executable of eternal programs that generate the datasets (e.g., `PartitionerTT` and `Partitioner`). Parallelism in the application is exploited during the execution of the `foreach` loop that, as the `for` loop in JS4Cloud, is executed in parallel on each element of the dataset array (lines 20–23 and 26–28). In fact, similarly to the JS4Cloud `for` statement, a `foreach` statement in Swift applies its body of statements to elements of an array in a fully concurrent, pipelined manner, as they are set to a value.

As we can see from the manner in which this application example is programmed, although syntax is different is several aspects, the programming style of the Swift language is similar to the J4Cloud programming style. Also the data driven approach and the exploitation of parallelism is similar in the two languages.

## 4.5 SUMMARY

In the latest years new commercial and research-oriented software tools and frameworks have been designed, implemented, and used for executing data analysis applications on clouds systems. This chapter focused on a selection of those frameworks and discussed their main features, architectures, and programming approaches. Among those systems we mention here Pegasus, Hunk, BigML, Swift, DMCF, Mahout, and Spark. Since a deep description of how all the systems can be used for implementing data analysis applications could not be accommodated in this chapter, we focused on one of them, the DMCF environment, and discussed its cloud-based software architecture, how it implements scalability of data analysis applications, and presented solutions that have been adopted for its implementation on a public cloud.

The DMCF system offers two high-level programming languages for developing data analysis workflows that can be executed in parallel on a cloud. *VL4Cloud* (Visual Language for Cloud), a visual language that lets users develop applications by programming the workflow component graphically, and *JS4Cloud* (JavaScript for Cloud), a scripting language based on JavaScript designed for programming data analysis workflows. Both languages have been presented and compared. In particular, language patterns and constructs for the exploitation of parallelism on data analysis applications have been described. A few programming examples using the key programming abstractions (*Data* elements to denote files and storage elements, and *Tool* elements to denote algorithms, software tools and applications executed on *Data* elements) have been illustrated and discussed.

The final section of the chapter has been devoted to four significant case studies of data analysis. Trajectory mining, ensemble learning, and parallel classification based on a MapReduce-workflow hybrid approach have been discussed. Finally, a comparison between JS4Cloud and Swift is done through the programming of a parallel classification workflow. The contents of this chapter can be a useful contribution for learning how scalable solutions for data analysis can be designed and used. Through the analysis and presentation of some of the most advanced tools in this area, it is possible to understand how cloud solutions can effectively support the development of complex and compute intensive big data analysis.

## REFERENCES

Altomare, A., Cesario, E., Comito, C., Marozzo, F., Talia, D., 2014. Trajectory pattern mining over a cloud-based framework for urban computing. Proceedings of the Sixteenth International Conference on High Performance Computing and Communications (HPCC 2014), Paris, France, pp. 367–374, IEEE.

Anil, R., Owen, S., Dunning, T., Friedman, E., 2012. Mahout in action. Manning, Shelter Island, NY.

Ball, M., Barnhart, C., Dresner, M., Hansen, M., Neels, K., Odoni, A., Peterson, E., Sherry, L., Trani, A.A., Zou, B., 2010. Total delay impact study: a comprehensive assessment of the costs and impacts of flight delay in the United States. NEXTOR Final Report prepared for the Federal Aviation Administration.

Bharathi, S., Chervenak, A., Deelman, E., Mehta, G., Su, M.-H., Vahi. K., 2008. Characterization of scientific workflows. In: Workflows in Support of Large-Scale Science. WORKS 2008. Third Workshop, pp. 1–10.

Deelman, E., Gannon, D., Shields, M., Taylor, I., 2009. Workflows and e-science: an overview of workflow system features and capabilities. Future Gener. Comput. Syst. 25 (5), 528–540.

Deelman, E., Vahi, K., Juve, G., Rynge, M., Callaghan, S., Maechling, P.J., Mayani, R., Chen, W., Ferreira da Silva, R., Livny, M., Wenger, K., 2015. Pegasus: a workflow management system for science automation. Future Gener. Comput. Syst. 46, 17–35.

Giardine, B., et al., 2005. Galaxy: a platform for interactive large-scale genome analysis. Genome Res. 15, 1451–1455.

Gu, Yunhong, Grossman, Robert L., 2009. Sector and sphere: the design and implementation of high-performance data cloud. Philos. Trans. A. Math. Phys. Eng. Sci. 367 (1897), 2429–2445.

Hall, M., Frank, E., Holmes, G., Pfahringer, B., Reutemann, P., Witten, I.H., 2009. The weka data mining software: an update. SIGKDD Explor. Newsl. 11 (1), 10–18.

Juve, G., Deelman, E., Vahi, K., Mehta, G., Berriman, B., Berman, B.P., Maechling, P., 2010. Data Sharing Options for Scientific Workflows on Amazon EC2. Int. Conference on High Performance Computing, Networking, Storage and Analysis (SC 2010).

Kranjc, J., Podpecan,V., Lavrac, N., 2012. ClowdFlows: a cloud based scientific workflow platform In: Machine Learning and Knowledge Discovery in Databases, ser. Lecture Notes in Computer Science, vol. 7524. Springer, Heidelberg, Germany, pp. 816–819.

Kuncheva, L.I., 2004. Combining Pattern Classifiers: Methods and Algorithms. Wiley-Interscience. Chichester.

Marozzo, F., Talia, D., Trunfio, P., 2015. JS4Cloud: script-based workflow programming for scalable data analysis on cloud platforms. Concurrency and Computation: Practice and Experience, Wiley InterScience. Chichester.

Nagavaram, A., Agrawal, G., Freitas, M., Mehta, G., Mayani, R., Deelman, E., 2011. A cloud-based dynamic workflow for mass spectrometry data analysis. In: Proceedings of the Seventh IEEE International Conference on e-Science (e-Science 2011).

Quinlan, J.R., 1993. C4.5: Programs for Machine Learning. Morgan Kaufmann Publishers Inc. San Francisco, CA.

Shahrivari, S., 2014. Beyond batch processing: towards real-time and streaming big data. Computers 3 (4), 117–129.

Wilde, M., Hategan, M., Wozniak, J.M., Clifford, B., Katz, D.S., Foster, I., 2011. Swift: a language for distributed parallel scripting. Parallel Comput. 37 (9), 633–652.

Wozniak, J.M., Wilde, M., Foster, I.T., 2014. Language features for scalable distributed-memory dataflow computing. In: Proceedings of Data-flow Execution Models for Extreme-scale Computing at PACT.

Xin, R.S., Rosen, J., Zaharia, M., Franklin, M.J., Shenker, S., Stoica. I., 2013. Shark: SQL and rich analytics at scale. In: Proceedings of the 2013 ACM SIGMOD International Conference on Management of Data (SIGMOD '13). New York, USA.

Zhou, Z.-H., Li, M., 2010. Semi-supervised learning by disagreement. Knowl. Inf. Syst. 24 (3), 415–439.

# CHAPTER 5

# Research Trends in Big Data Analysis

Big data analysis is a very active research area with significant impact on industrial and scientific domains, where is important to analyze very large and complex data repositories. In particular, in many cases, data to be analyzed are stored in cloud platforms and elastic computing clouds facilities are exploited to speedup the analysis. This chapter outlines and discusses main research trends in big data analytics and cloud systems for managing and mining large-scale data repositories. Topics and trends in the areas of exascale computing and social data analysis are reported. Section 5.1 discusses issues and challenges for implementing massively parallel and/or distributed applications in the area of big data analysis on exascale systems. Section 5.2 discusses recent trends in social data analysis, with a focus on mining mobility patterns from large volumes of trajectory data from online social network data. Finally, Section 5.3 discusses key research areas for the implementation of scalable data analytics dealing with huge, distributed data sources.

## 5.1 DATA-INTENSIVE EXASCALE COMPUTING

Computer system performance and storage capacity have increased very significantly in the past decades. This prodigious growth has powered many innovations across all sectors of our society. New advances in biology and medicine, physics and engineering, energy, goods design and manufacturing, transportation, environmental modeling, Internet services, financial analysis, and social media mainly depend on unceasing rises in computer performance and data storage.

In this scenario, the design of exascale computers is a very significant research challenge that is under investigation in the timeframe 2010–2020 with the goal of building computers composed of a large number of multicore processors (with more than 100 cores per chip) expected to deliver a performance of $10^{18}$ operations per second.

From a software point of view, these new computing platforms open big issues and challenges for software tools and environments and runtime systems that must be able to manage a high degree of parallelism and data locality. Additionally, to provide efficient methods for storing, accessing, and communicating data, intelligent techniques for data analysis and scalable software architectures enabling the scalable extraction of useful information and knowledge from data, are needed. Moreover, exascale systems and models are required to design and implement massively parallel and/or distributed algorithms and applications in the area of big data analysis. This trend needs new models and technologies for enabling cloud computing systems, HPC architectures and extreme scale platforms to support the implementation of clever data analysis algorithms that ought to be scalable and dynamic in resource usage.

Complex data analysis tasks involve data- and compute-intensive algorithms. These algorithms require large and efficient storage facilities together with high-performance processors. In this setting, exascale-computing infrastructures will play the role of an impressive platform for addressing both the computational and data storage needs of big data analysis applications. However, as aforementioned, in order to have a complete scenario, efforts must be performed for implementing big data analytics algorithms, architectures, programming tools, and applications in exascale systems.

We expect that data analytics systems on large-scale clouds and massively parallel systems will become common platforms for big data analytics within a few years. As new computing infrastructures will become common scalable platforms for big data analytics, programming tools suites, and data mining strategies will be ported on such platforms for developing big data discovery solutions. In particular, the exploitation of the distributed workflow paradigm in the area of big data analytics will result in scalable solutions for big data analysis. Since offering data analysis as a service appears to be a viable approach to implement pervasive big data applications, the exploitation of exascale scalable computing platform will provide the appropriate infrastructure for such service delivery.

## 5.1.1 Exascale Scalability in Data Analysis
As discussed in the previous chapters, data analysis gained importance because of the large and pervasive availability of data sources and the

continuous enhancements of techniques and algorithms to find insights in them. As a matter of fact, as data analysis technology advances, exploiting the power of data analytics is restructuring several scientific and industrial sectors. The amount of data that social networks daily generate is just one example of this trend. About 100 TB of data is uploaded daily to Facebook and Twitter. These notable amounts of data streams show that it is vital to design scalable solutions to process and analyze massive datasets. As a general forecast, some experts estimate data generated to reach about 45 ZB worldwide by 2020.

There is a large consensus on the fact that scalability and performance requirements are challenging conventional data storage, file systems, and database management systems. Architectures of such systems have reached some limits in handling very large processing tasks involving petabytes of data because they have not been built for scaling. This scenario demands for new architectures and solutions for implementing analytics platforms that must process big data for extracting complex knowledge models. Exascale systems, both from the hardware and the software side, can play a key role to support solutions for these problems. Indeed, many applications require the use of scalable data analysis platforms. A well-known example is the ATLAS detector from the Large Hadron Collider at CERN in Geneva. The ATLAS infrastructure has a capacity of 200 PB of disk and 300,000 cores, with more than 100 computing centers connected via 10 Gbps links. The data collection rate is very high and ATLAS actually only records a fraction of the data produced by the collider. Different teams of scientists run complex applications to analyze portions of those huge volumes of data. This analysis would be impossible without a high-performance infrastructure that supports data storage, communication, and processing. Astronomy is another good example of the massive data amounts that today are collected for scientific analysis. Computational astronomers are collecting and producing larger and larger datasets each year that without scalable infrastructures cannot be managed and processed.

If we move from science to society, we can consider social data and e-health. Social networks, such as Facebook and Twitter, have become very popular and are receiving increasing attention from the research community since, through the huge amount of user-generated data, they provide precious information concerning human dynamics and behaviors. When the volume of data to be analyzed is of the order of terabytes or petabytes (billions of Tweets or posts), scalable storage and computing solutions must be used. The same occurs in the e-health domain, where huge amounts of patient data are available and can be used for improving therapies, for forecasting and tracking of health data, for the management of hospitals and health centers, for improving patient understanding, and/or physician-patient communication with analytics.

### 5.1.2  Programming Issues for Exascale Data Analysis

Implementing scalable data analysis applications in exascale computing systems is a complex job, which requires high level fine-grained parallel constructs and skills in parallel and distributed programming. In particular, mechanisms and expertise are needed to express task dependencies and intertask parallelism, to use mechanisms of synchronization, load balancing, and to properly manage the memory and the communication among a very large number of tasks. Moreover, if the computing infrastructures are heterogeneous and require different libraries and tools to program applications on them, the problems are even more complex. To cope with all these issues, different scalable programming models have been proposed to write data-intensive applications (Diaz et al., 2012).

Scalable programming models may be categorized based on their level of abstraction (high- and low-level scalable models) and on how they allow programmers to create applications (visual or code-based formalisms). Using high-level scalable models, a programmer defines only the high-level logic of an application, while the low-level details that are not essential for application design are hidden, including infrastructure dependent execution details. The programmer is helped in application definition, and application performance depends on the compiler that analyzes the application code and optimizes its execution on the underlying infrastructure.

Instead, low-level scalable models allow the programmers to interact directly with computing and storage elements of the underlying infrastructure and thus to define the applications parallelism directly. In this case, programming an application requires more skills, and the application performance strongly depends on the quality of the code written by the programmer.

Data analysis applications can be designed through a visual interface, which is a convenient design approach for high-level users, for example, domain-expert analysts having a limited understanding of programming. In addition, a visual representation of workflows intrinsically captures parallelism at the task level, without the need to make parallelism explicit through control structures (Maheshwari and Montagnat, 2010). Code-based formalism allows users to program complex applications more rapidly, in a more concise way, and with higher flexibility (Marozzo et al., 2015). The code-base applications can be designed in different ways:

* With a language or an extension of language that allows to express parallel applications;
* With annotations in the application code that allow the compiler to identify which instructions will be executed in parallel; and
* Using a library in the application code that adds parallelism to application.

Given the variety of data analysis applications and types of users (from end users to skilled programmers) that can be envisioned in future exascale systems, there will be a need for scalable programming models with different levels of abstractions (high- and low-level) and different design formalisms (visual- and code-based), according to the aforementioned classification. Thus, the programming models should adapt to user needs by ensuring a good trade-off between ease in defining applications and efficiency of executing them on exascale architectures composed by a massive number of processors.

Data-intensive applications are software programs that have a significant need to process large volumes of data (Gorton et al., 2008). Such applications devote most of their processing time to run I/O operations, exchange, and move data among the processing elements of a parallel computing infrastructure. Parallel processing of data analysis applications typically involves accessing, preprocessing, partitioning, aggregating, querying, mining, and visualizing data that can be processed independently. These operations are executed using application programs running in parallel on a scalable computing platform that can be a large cloud system or an exascale machine composed of many thousands of processors. In particular, the main challenges for programming data analysis applications on exascale computing systems come from the potential scalability and resilience of mechanisms and operations made available to developers for accessing and managing data. Indeed, processing very large data volumes requires operations and new algorithms, that are able to scale in loading, storing, and processing massive amounts of data that generally must be partitioned in very small data grains, on which analysis is done by thousands to millions of simple parallel operations.

Evolutionary models have been recently proposed that extend or adapt traditional parallel programming models, such as MPI, OpenMP, and MapReduce (e.g., Pig Latin) to limit the communication overhead in message passing paradigms or to limit the synchronization control, if shared-models languages are used (Gropp and Snir, 2013). On the other hand, new models, languages and APIs based on a revolutionary approach, such as X10, ECL, GA, SHMEM, UPC, and Chapel have been implemented. These novel parallel paradigms are devised to address the requirements of massive parallelism. Languages such as X10, UPC, GA, and Chapel are based on a partitioned global address space (PGAS) memory model that can be suited to implement data-intensive exascale applications because it uses private data structures and limits the amount of shared data among parallel threads. Together with different approaches, such as Pig Latin and ECL, those models must be further investigated and adapted to provide data-centric scalable programming models useful to support the efficient implementation of exascale data analysis applications composed of up to millions of computing units, which process small data elements and exchange them with a very limited set of processing elements.

A scalable programming model based on basic operations for data intensive/data-driven applications must include operations for parallel data access, data-driven local communication, data processing on limited groups of cores, near-data synchronization, in-memory querying, group-level data aggregation, and locality-based data selection and classification. An efficient model must be able to manage a very large amount of parallelism, implement-reduced communication, and synchronization.

Supporting efficient data-intensive applications on exascale systems will require an accurate modeling of basic operations and th programming languages/APIs that will include them. At the same time, a significant programming effort of developers will be needed to implement complex algorithms and data-driven applications such as those used, for example, in big data analysis and distributed data mining. Programmers must be able to design and implement scalable algorithms by using the operations sketched above. To reach this goal, a coordinated effort between the operation/language designers and the application developers would be very fruitful.

At the exascale scale, the cost of accessing, moving, and processing data across a parallel system is enormous. This requires mechanisms, techniques and operations for efficient data access, placement and querying. In addition, scalable operations must be designed in such a way so as to avoid global synchronizations, centralized control, and global communications. Many data scientists want to be abstracted away from these tricky and lower level aspects of HPC until at least they have their code working and then potentially to tweak communication and distribution choices in a high level manner, in order to further tune their code. Interoperability and integration with the MapReduce model and MPI must be investigated with the main goal of achieving scalability on large-scale data processing.

Different data-centric abstractions can be integrated in order to provide a unified programming model and API that allow the efficient programming of large-scale heterogeneous and distributed memory systems. A software implementation can be developed as a library. Its application to reference data-intensive benchmarks allows gathering feedback that will lead to improvements in the prototype. In order to simplify the development of applications in heterogeneous distributed memory environments, large-scale data-parallelism can be exploited on top of the abstraction of $n$-dimensional arrays subdivided in tiles, so that different tiles are placed on different computing nodes that process in parallel the tiles they own. Such an approach allows one to easily process the tiles at each node in either regular CPUs or in any of the heterogeneous systems available (GPUs, Xeon Phi coprocessors, etc.) using a unified API and runtime that hides the complexity of the underlying process.

Abstract data types provided by libraries, so that they can be easily integrated in existing applications, should support this abstraction.

As mentioned earlier, another issue is the gap between users with HPC needs and experts with the skills to make the most of these technologies. An appropriate directive-based approach can be to design, implement and evaluate a compiler framework that allows generic translations from high-level languages to exascale heterogeneous platforms. A programming model should be designed at a level that is higher than that of standards, such as OpenCL. The model should enable the rapid development with reduced effort for different heterogeneous platforms, including low energy architectures and mobile devices.

## 5.2 MASSIVE SOCIAL NETWORK ANALYSIS

A huge amount of user-generated data in social networks can be exploited to extract valuable information concerning human dynamics and behaviors. Social data analysis is emerging as a fast growing research area, which is aimed at extracting useful information from this mass of data. It can be used for the analysis of collective sentiments to understanding the behavior of groups of people or the dynamics of public opinion.

One of the most interesting features of social networks is its ability to associate spatial context to social posts. For example, Twitter, Facebook, Flickr, and Instagram, exploit the GPS readings of mobile phones to tag Tweets, posts, and photos with geographical coordinates. Therefore, social network users traveling through sets of locations, produce a huge amount of geo-location data that embed extensive knowledge about human dynamics and mobility behaviors. The potential to harness rich information provided by geo-tagged social data may impact many areas including urban planning, intelligent traffic management, route recommendations, security, and health monitoring.

In the past few years, many studies have been carried out regarding the extraction of trajectories from geo-tagged social data (Zheng, 2015). Compared to trajectory pattern mining from GPS data (Giannotti et al., 2007), extracting trajectories from social network data is a more challenging task because data from location-based social networks are often sparse and irregular, in contrast to GPS traces of mobile devices, which are highly available and sampled at regular time intervals.

In most cases, geo-tagged data from social networks provide positioning information of a huge number of users, but information about each user is limited to very few positions per day. Therefore, trajectories are usually generated at low or irregular frequency, thereby leaving the routes between two consecutive points of a single trajectory uncertain.

A research stream in this area focuses on identifying hot spots and tourist routine behaviors from global collection of geo-referenced photos. Photo-sharing social networks contain billions of publicly accessible images that are taken virtually everywhere on earth. These photos are annotated with various forms of information including geo-spatial and textual metadata. For example, Yin et al. (2011) exploited Flickr data to identify the most frequent travel routes and the top interesting locations in a given geo-spatial region. This was obtained by associating semantics to the locations based on the tags given to each photo by Flickr users.

Another approach for trajectory mining from social network data consists of exploiting only spatio-temporal information, without leveraging image features and tag-based data. Comito et al., (2015) analyzed the time- and geo-referenced information associated with Twitter data, in order to detect typical trajectories and discover common behavior, that is, patterns, rules, and regularities in moving trajectories. The basic assumption is that people often tend to follow common routes: for example, they go to work every day traveling the same roads. Thus, if we have enough data to model typical behaviors, such knowledge can be used to predict and manage future movements of people. In particular, the goal of this work was to provide top interesting spots and frequent travel sequences among locations in a given geo-spatial region. Interesting locations include popular tourist destinations and commonly frequented public areas, such as shopping malls/streets, restaurants, and cinemas.

Given the large amount of data to process, the methodology proposed by Comito et al. (2015) consists of various phases allowing the collection of Tweets, detect locations from them, identify travel routes between such locations, mine frequent travel routes using sequential pattern mining, and extract spatial-temporal information for each of those routes to capture the factors that might drive users' movements. As a case study, the methodology was applied to a large set of Tweets posted within the city of London. The analysis distinguishes among routes involving multiple people and routes taken by a single person. Collective routes indicate crowd mobility and also how people behave in the city, whereas individual routes characterize a given person, highlighting her/his daily mobility patterns and providing insights about her/his daily routines.

Even though trajectory information extracted from geo-tagged data are indicative of a user's behavior, it lacks some semantics about the type of place where a user is (e.g., home, office, museum), which would allow a better understanding of users' patterns. Some location-based social network services (e.g., Foursquare) allow each user to explicitly indicate the place category she/he is at. Although the category information is very rich and can enable more refined applications, this is a manual process, in which the user is voluntarily "checking into" a place. In other social networking tools, a location is simply represented as latitude-longitude coordinates automatically associated to a post by the service. However, knowing the semantics of the type of place a user is at can be potentially very useful. It could allow inferring users' common interests, improving activity prediction, and enabling mobile user recommendation and advertisement. Falcone et al. (2014) defined a method to extract spatial-temporal patterns from geo-Tweets exploiting a number of features specific to the places, duration of the stay, time of day and of week of the typical stay, number of visitors and the regularity of their behavior in the place. Another work that identifies place category from social network data is the one by Ye et al. (2011), which derived eight place label categories from Whrrl, a location-based social network. They used a support vector machine on features such as check-in frequency and time of day to label over 53,000 places from almost 6,000 users.

The work by Cesario et al. (2015) is an example on how social networks can be exploited to analyze the behavior of large groups of people attending popular events. The goal was to monitor the attendance of Twitter users during the FIFA World Cup 2014 matches to discover the most frequent movements of fans during the competition. The data source is represented by all geo-tagged Tweets collected during the 6 matches of the World Cup from June 12, 2014 to July 13, 2014. For each match, only the geo-tagged Tweets whose coordinates fell within the area of stadiums, during the matches, were considered. Then, trajectory pattern mining analysis on the set of Tweets considered was carried out. The analysis is based on the search of frequent item sets that allow identifying the groups of matches attended most frequently by spectators. Original results were obtained in terms of number of matches attended by groups of fans, clusters of most attended matches, and most frequented stadiums. The number of Tweets posted from inside the stadiums during the soccer matches was pretty high (about half a milion), allowing their analysis with well-known data mining techniques, such as the Apriori algorithm, for frequent itemsets computing and association rules discovery. The methodology adopted to carry out this data analysis task could be adopted in similar scenarios, where groups of people attend social events to understand collective behaviors that are very hard to discover with traditional social analysis techniques.

Cloud systems can be effectively exploited to support trajectory-mining applications from social network data, such as those described previously, or from other data sources (e.g., open data). The application by Altomare et al. (2014), introduced in Section 4.4.1, demonstrates the benefits derived from the use of big data solutions for trajectory mining in urban computing and smart city applications. Urban computing is the process of acquisition, integration, and analysis of big and heterogeneous urban data to tackle major issues that cities face today, including air pollution, energy consumption, traffic flows, human mobility, environmental preservation, commercial activities, and savings in public spending. In urban computing scenarios, clouds can play an essential role by helping city administrators to quickly acquire new capabilities and reduce initial capital costs by means of a comprehensive pay-as-you-go solution. In fact, by providing applications, infrastructure, networking, systems software, middleware, and maintenance, cloud computing lowers the barrier of entry and enables city managers to deliver high quality services to their citizens. In addition, managing heterogeneous data volumes while allowing interoperability among different tools, also needs compliance to standards. In this regard, cloud computing systems are suitable platforms to fulfill most of the above requirements, due to their features such as scalable computing, on-demand processing, facilitating data accessibility, and storage across platforms.

Several cloud-enabled tools for urban planning and management, proposed so far, demonstrate the important role of cloud computing in this area. Environmental Software and Services (ESS) exploits the cloud paradigm to offer a range of services for environmental planning and management,[1] policy, and decision making world wide. Analogously, the Environmental Virtual Observatory pilot (EVOp) uses clouds to achieve similar objectives in the soil and water domains.[2] The European Platform for Intelligent Cities (EPIC) combines a cloud computing infrastructure with the knowledge and expertise of the Living Lab approach to deliver sustainable,[3] user-driven Web services for citizens and businesses. The Life 2.0 project offers a set of services ranging from basic geographical positioning systems to socially networked services and to local market-based services.[4] The project aims to provide solutions that increase opportunities for social contacts among elderly people in their local area, by providing new services based on the use of tracking systems and social network applications. Finally, IBM introduced Smarter City Solutions on the IBM SmartCloud Enterprise,[5] a public cloud platform that includes hardware, network, and storage. The platform provides pay-as-you-go services for urban management within cities Those services include application software, infrastructure, networking, systems software, middleware, and maintenance.

## 5.3  KEY RESEARCH AREAS

As discussed in the previous sections, scalable data analytics require high-level and easy-to-use design tools for programming large applications dealing with huge, distributed data sources. This necessitates further research and development in several key areas such as:

- *Programming models for big data analytics*: big data analytics programming tools require novel complex abstract structures. The MapReduce model is often used on clusters and clouds, but more research is needed to develop scalable high-level models and tools. State-of-the-art solutions generated major success stories, however

---

[1]www.ess.co.at

[2]www.evo-uk.org

[3]www.epic-cities.eu

[4]www.life2project.eu

[5]www-01.ibm.com/software/industry/smartercities-on-cloud

they are not mature and suffer several problems from data transfer bottlenecks to performance unpredictability.

• *Data and tool interoperability and openness*: interoperability is a main issue in large-scale applications that use resources such as data and computing nodes. Standard formats and models are needed to support interoperability and ease cooperation among teams using different data formats and tools.

• *Integration of big data analytics frameworks*: the service-oriented paradigm allows running large-scale distributed workflows on heterogeneous platforms along with software components developed using different programming languages or tools.

• *Scalable software architectures for fine grain in-memory data access and analysis*: exascale processors and storage devices must be exploited with fine-grain runtime models. Software solutions to handle many cores on processors and scalable processor-to-processor communications have to be designed to exploit exascale hardware.

• *Tools for massive social network analysis*: the effective analysis of social network data on a large scale requires new software tools for real-time data extraction and mining, using cloud services and high-performance computing approaches. Social data streaming analysis tools represent very useful technologies to understand collective behaviors from social media data.

*Tools for data exploration and model visualization*: new approaches for data exploration and model visualization are necessary, taking into account the size of data and complexity of the knowledge extracted. As data grow bigger, visualization tools will become more useful to summarize and show them in a compact and easy-to-see way.

*Local mining and distributed model combination*: as big data applications often involve several local sources and distributed coordination, collecting distributed data sources into a centralized server for analysis, is neither practical nor possible. Scalable data analysis systems have to enable local mining of data sources, model exchange, and fusion mechanisms to compose the results produced in the distributed nodes (Wu et al., 2014). According to this approach, the global analysis can be performed by distributing local mining and supporting the global combination of every local knowledge to generate the complete model.

- *In-memory analysis:* most of the data analysis tools query data sources on disks while, differently from those, in-memory analytics query data in main memory (RAM). This approach brings many benefits in terms of query speed up and faster decisions. In-memory databases are, for example, very effective in real-time data analysis, but they require high-performance hardware support and fine-grain parallel algorithms. New 64-bit operating systems allow addressing memory, up to 1 TB, making it realistic to cache a very large amount of data in RAM. Hence, this research area is very promising.

## 5.4 SUMMARY

The field of big data analysis is a very active research discipline that has significant impact on industrial and scientific processes and applications. In many cases, big data are stored and analyzed in cloud platforms. In this chapter two research areas, exascale computing and social data analysis, have been discussed and a few key research topics that need to be deeply investigated in the future to find solutions for the implementation of scalable data analytics on huge and distributed data sources have been outlined.

In particular, the development of exascale computers is a very significant research challenge that is under investigation with the goal of building computers composed of up to hundreds of thousands cores for delivering a performance of $10^{18}$ operations per second. From a software point of view, these new computing platforms open big issues and challenges for software tools, environments, and runtime systems that must be able to manage a high degree of parallelism and data locality. Moreover, efficient methods to store, access, communicate, and mine data are needed. When those methods will be designed and implemented, exascale systems will be used to implement massively parallel and distributed applications in the area of big data analysis.

On the other side, social data analysis is emerging as a fast growing research area aimed at extracting useful information from data directly provided by people. It can be used for the analysis of collective sentiments, for understanding the behavior of groups of people, or the dynamics of public opinion. In this chapter, we introduced the main issues that are addressed in this area for developing scalable data analysis by exploiting cloud computing features and discussed some recent research contributions that show how social data analysis can be carried out in smart city and urban computing applications.

The eight key research areas listed in the previous section represent important research topics, which are very promising for researchers and professionals working in the area of cloud-based data analysis. Future solutions that will be created in these areas will have significant impact on the development of big data analysis frameworks and applications in the next decade.

## REFERENCES

Altomare, A., Cesario, E., Comito, C., Marozzo, F., Talia, D., 2014. Trajectory pattern mining over a Cloud-based framework for urban computing. In: Proceedings of the 16th International Conference on High Performance Computing and Communications (HPCC 2014), IEEE, Paris, France, pp. 367–374.

Cesario, E., Congedo, C., Marozzo, F., Riotta, G., Spada, A., Talia, D., Trunfio, P., Turri, C., 2015. Following soccer fans from geotagged tweets at FIFA world cup 2014. In: Proceedings of the 2nd IEEE Conference on Spatial Data Mining and Geographical Knowledge Services (ICSDM 2015), Fuzhou, China, pp. 33–38.

Comito, C., Falcone, D., Talia, D., 2015. Mining popular travel routes from social network geotagged data. In: Damiani, E., Howlett, R.J., Jain, L.C., Gallo, L., De Pietro, G. (Eds.), Intelligent interactive multimedia systems and services, pp. 81–95.

Diaz, J., Munoz-Caro, C., Nino, A., 2012. A survey of parallel programming models and tools in the multi and many-core era. IEEE Trans. Parallel Distr. Syst. 23 (8), 1369–1386.

Falcone, D., Mascolo, C., Comito, C., Talia, D., Crowcroft, J., 2014. What is this place? Inferring place categories through user patterns identification in geo-tagged tweets. In: Proceedings of the International Conference on Mobile Computing, Applications, and Services (MobiCASE 2014), Austin, TX, USA.

Giannotti, F., Nanni, M., Pinelli, F., Pedreschi, D., 2007. Trajectory pattern mining. In: Proceedings of the Thirteenth ACM SIGKDD International Conference on Knowledge Discovery and Data Mining (KDD '07). ACM, New York, NY, USA, pp. 330–339.

Gorton, I., Greenfield, P., Szalay, A.S., Williams, R., 2008. Data-intensive computing in the 21st century. IEEE Comput. 41 (4), 30–32.

Gropp, W., Snir, M., 2013. Programming for exascale computers. Comput. Sci. Eng. 15 (6), 7–35.

Maheshwari, K., Montagnat, J., 2010. Scientific work flow development using both visual and script-based representation. In: Proceedings of the 6th World Congress on Services, SERVICES 0, Washington, DC, USA, pp. 328–335.

Marozzo, F., Talia, D., Trunfio, P., 2015. JS4Cloud: Script-Based Workflow Programming for Scalable Data Analysis on Cloud Platforms. Concurrency and Computation: Practice and Experience. Wiley InterScience, Chichester.

Wu, X., Zhu, X., Wu, G.-Q., Ding, W., 2014. Data mining with big data. IEEE Trans. Knowledge Data Eng. 26 (1), 97–107.

Ye, M., Shou, D., Lee, W.-C., Yin, P., Janowicz, K., 2011. On the semantic annotation of places in location-based social networks, In: Proceedings of the 17th ACM SIGKDD International Conference on Knowledge Discovery and Data Mining (KDD 2011), San Diego, CA, pp. 520–528.

Yin, Z., Cao, L., Han, J., Luo, J., Huang, T.S., 2011. Diversified trajectory pattern ranking in geotagged social media, In: Proceedings of the 11th SIAM International Conference on Data Mining (SDM 2011), Mesa, AZ, pp. 980–991.

Zheng, Y., 2015. Trajectory data mining: an overview. ACM Trans. Intel. Syst. Technol. 6 (3), 1–41.

Printed in the United States
By Bookmasters